Workbook

business EXPERT

Wirtschaft & Verwaltung

von
David Christie
Ephrem Wellenbrock

Ernst Klett Verlag
Stuttgart · Leipzig

Workbook
business EXPERT
Wirtschaft und Verwaltung

Autoren: David Christie, Oxford; Ephrem Wellenbrock, Dorsten (Prüfungen)

Berater: Hans-Henning Jasper, Gunhild Lehmkuhl, Georg Mandt, Bernd Deininghaus, Anja Kobus, Monika Schumacher, Elke Uthoff

Werkübersicht:
Schülerbuch, 978-3-12-800111-1
Lehrerhandbuch, mit Lehrer-Service-CD-ROM und 2 Audio-CDs, 978-3-12-800113-5
Workbook mit Prüfungsvorbereitung, 978-3-12-800112-8

1. Auflage 1 5 4 3 2 1 | 13 12 11 10 09

Alle Drucke dieser Auflage sind unverändert und können im Unterricht nebeneinander verwendet werden.
Die letzte Zahl bezeichnet das Jahr des Druckes.

Projektleitung: Matthias Rupp
Redaktion: Chris Caridia, Publishing Services, Berlin;
Herstellung: Angelika Lindner

Gestaltung: B2 Büro für Gestaltung, Andreas Staiger, Stuttgart
Umschlaggestaltung: B2 Büro für Gestaltung, Andreas Staiger, Stuttgart
Illustrationen: Jeongsook Lee, Köln; Andreas Staiger, Stuttgart
Satz: B2 Büro für Gestaltung, Andreas Staiger, Petra Staisch, Stuttgart
Reproduktion: Meyle + Müller Medien-Management, Pforzheim
Druck: Mediahaus Biering GmbH, München

Printed in Germany
ISBN 978-3-12-800112-8

9 783128 001128

Zeichenerklärung

→ SB: S. 14–15	Verweise auf das Schülerbuch
→ GS: H1, H2	Verweise auf das Grammar Summary im Schülerbuch
EXTRA	Vertiefungsaufgaben u.a. zum Wortschatz und zur Sprachmittlung
Video lounge	vertieftes Seh-/Hörverstehenstraining
More listening practice	Verweis auf vertieftes Hörverstehenstraining
ROUNDUP	Zusammenfassung der Business Communication

Language check

Dieser 'Preliminary Test' ist weder eine Prüfung noch eine Klausur! Ziel des Tests ist es, IHNEN die Möglichkeit zu geben, Ihre Englischkenntnisse besser einschätzen zu können.
Lösen Sie bitte alle Aufgaben des Tests und vergleichen Sie dann erst Ihre Lösungen mit denen des Lösungshefts. Sollten Sie eventuell auf dem einen oder anderen Gebiet (z. B. bei den Verbzeiten oder beim Grundwortschatz) Schwächen entdecken, finden Sie dazu Tipps, wie Sie diese ausräumen können.
Viel Spaß und Erfolg!

A Leseverstehen

Lesen Sie den Text und beantworten Sie auf Deutsch die Fragen auf der nächsten Seite. Schreiben Sie Ihre Antworten auf ein Blatt Papier.

Simon's business

Simon lives in England and runs his own e-commerce business. He has done this now for two years, and things are going well. This is the story of how he began ...

After Simon left school five years ago, he studied for two years at a vocational college in Birmingham, Britain's second largest city. Simon's course was about computers and IT. He got his college qualification, and then he started work in a company in his hometown. The company imported and sold clothes. Simon looked after the company's computer network and all its IT.

A part of Simon's job was also to buy computer equipment and he noticed that one thing he bought often was blank DVDs. The company backed up its data on these, and Simon bought a hundred or more each month. He also knew that at home he used a lot of blank DVDs to burn and save movies and his downloaded music.

Simon always thought when he bought DVDs that the price was very high. So he spent some time on the internet and found out quickly that blank DVDs were much cheaper in America. That is when he had his business idea. If he bought DVDs in the States, he could sell them in the UK at a profit and still be cheaper than lots of other DVD sellers. He decided to start his own business.

Simon did some more research on the internet and found that most businesses and individuals bought blank DVDs online. Around 87% of all blank DVD sales were over the internet. He therefore decided that his company would also be an e-commerce company. The big advantage of this was that he would not need a shop. He only needed a warehouse where he could store DVDs until he sent them to his customers by post. He looked around and after two weeks he found the ideal place: a warehouse on the outskirts of Birmingham which he could rent for £600 per month.

Simon contacted a number of blank DVD suppliers in the USA and finally found one that he thought would be a good business partner. This person would sell Simon blank DVDs at a good price and in large quantities.

Simon was now ready to start his business but there was one more important thing to do. He needed some capital – money that he could use during the first few months to buy DVDs and to rent the warehouse until people began buying his products. Simon wrote a careful business plan and took it to his bank. The plan showed all his calculations and explained how the business would work. The bank thought that Simon had a good idea and they gave him a loan of £10,000. A month later a new company called 'Simon's DVDs' was online!

(471 words)

► **vocational college** *Berufsschule* ► **warehouse** *Lagerhalle* ► **loan** *Darlehen*

Fragen

1. Worin besteht Simons 'Business'? Was ist seine tägliche Arbeit?
2. Was machte Simon, bevor er sein Unternehmen gründete? Welche Ausbildung hatte er für diese Stelle absolviert?
3. Wie kam er auf seine Geschäftsidee?
4. Warum hat er sich für ein 'e-commerce' Geschäft entschieden?
5. Welche Kosten-Vorteile hatte diese Art von Unternehmen für Simon?
6. Warum musste er als ersten Schritt zur Bank gehen?
7. Wie hatte sich Simon auf das Gespräch mit seiner Bank vorbereitet? Was war das Ergebnis des Gesprächs?

B Zeiten und Formen des Verbs

1 **Complete the sentences with the correct forms of the verbs.**
Think about:
- **the tense *(Zeit)***
- **the form and spelling *(Schreibweise).***

1. Christian Rhien is a student at a German vocational college in Gelsenkirchen. He ______ **(start)** his course last year.
2. Christian is on a full-time course. He ______ **(have)** lessons every day. He usually ______ **(go)** to college by bike.
3. If all goes well, Christian hopes that in the future he ______ **(get)** a good job in an office.
4. Silvia Stoldt is also a vocational college student. She ______ **(not/live)** in Gelsenkirchen. She ______ **(come)** from Munster.
5. Silvia ______ **(begin)** her course last September. Before that she ______ **(be)** at a Realschule in Munster.
6. Jan Behling ______ **(finish)** his college course two years ago. For the last two years he ______ **(work)** in an office in his hometown of Frankfurt.
7. Jan likes his job a lot. Right now, it's 8.30 in the morning and he ______ **(talk)** to his work colleagues.
8. Last year, one of Jan's colleagues ______ **(spend)** six months in the USA. While he ______ **(live)** there, he ______ **(meet)** Carol. She's now his fiancée *(Verlobte)*.
9. What about you? ______ ever ______ **(you/be)** to the USA?
10. Would you like to visit the USA? Which American city would you visit if you ______ **(have)** the chance?

2 **Now complete these sentences with the correct forms and tenses of the verbs again.**

1. In his business, Simon sells DVDs. His DVDs ______ **(sell)** on the internet.
2. Last week he sent 100 DVDs to a customer in the Netherlands. The DVDs ______ . ______ **(send)** by post.
3. Simon hopes that in future, people in more European countries will buy his DVDs. He hopes that soon they ______ **(buy)** in France, Spain and Germany, too.

C Satzbau

1 **Bilden Sie aus folgenden Wörtern oder Wortgruppen Aussagesätze.**

1. town / went / I / yesterday / to
2. I / in / my homework / do / often / my room
3. Terje / at / is / music / listening / the / moment / to
4. train / Cologne station / will / the / at / leave / 06.45
5. because / Tim / like / he / I / is / so friendly
6. have / me / if / you / ring / problem / a

2 **Bilden Sie jetzt aus den Sätzen 1, 2 und 3 oben verneinte Sätze.**

BEISPIEL:
I live in Spain.
I don't live in Spain.

1.
2.
3.

3 **Stellen Sie die Fragen.**

BEISPIEL:
I live **in Dusseldorf**.
Where do you live?

1. He (= Jan) lives **in Gelsenkirchen**.
2. We ate **fish**.
3. I'll do my homework **tomorrow**.
4. I saw **Greg** yesterday.
5. She talked to her friend **because she needed help**.

D Grundwortschatz

1 **Which is the correct word – a, b or c?**

1. London is bigger ... Berlin.
   - ☐ **a** as
   - ☐ **b** than
   - ☐ **c** then

2. There's a big … between these two things.
   - ☐ **a** difference
   - ☐ **b** difficulty
   - ☐ **c** description

3. I don't understand. Can you … that?
   - ☐ **a** repair
   - ☐ **b** repeat
   - ☐ **c** reply

4. The telephone was an amazing …
   - ☐ **a** invitation
   - ☐ **b** instruction
   - ☐ **c** invention

5. I'm sorry, I can't … your name.
   - ☐ **a** remember
   - ☐ **b** remind
   - ☐ **c** report

6. Claudia isn't … home at the moment.
   - ☐ **a** to
   - ☐ **b** in
   - ☐ **c** at

7. The match will take … next week in Cologne.
   - ☐ **a** place
   - ☐ **b** part
   - ☐ **c** off

8. We must find a … to this problem quickly.
   - ☐ **a** success
   - ☐ **b** surprise
   - ☐ **c** solution

9. Jerry waited for us … the station.
   - ☐ **a** for
   - ☐ **b** in front of
   - ☐ **c** before

10. It *could* happen but it's not very …
   - ☐ **a** probable
   - ☐ **b** possible
   - ☐ **c** reasonable

E Schreiben (Sprachmittlung)

1 **Translate these sentences into English.**

1. Ich meine (denke/glaube), dass die Arbeitswelt *(the world of work)* sehr interessant ist.

   ____

2. Viele meiner Freunde arbeiten in Büros.

   ____

3. Nach meinem Abschluss *(exam)* möchte ich auch in einem Büro arbeiten.

   ____

4. Es ist heutzutage *(nowadays)* leicht, im Ausland zu arbeiten.

   ____

5. Ich reise gerne und vielleicht werde ich eines Tages *(one day)* in den USA oder in Großbritannien arbeiten.

   ____

   ____

6. Englisch ist manchmal schwierig! Es ist aber *(however)* sehr wichtig, die Sprache zu lernen. Englisch ist eine Weltsprache.

   ____

   ____

1 Preparing for the world of work

A Young experts talking

→ SB: S.6–7

1 **Write the names of the EU countries then complete the text below.**

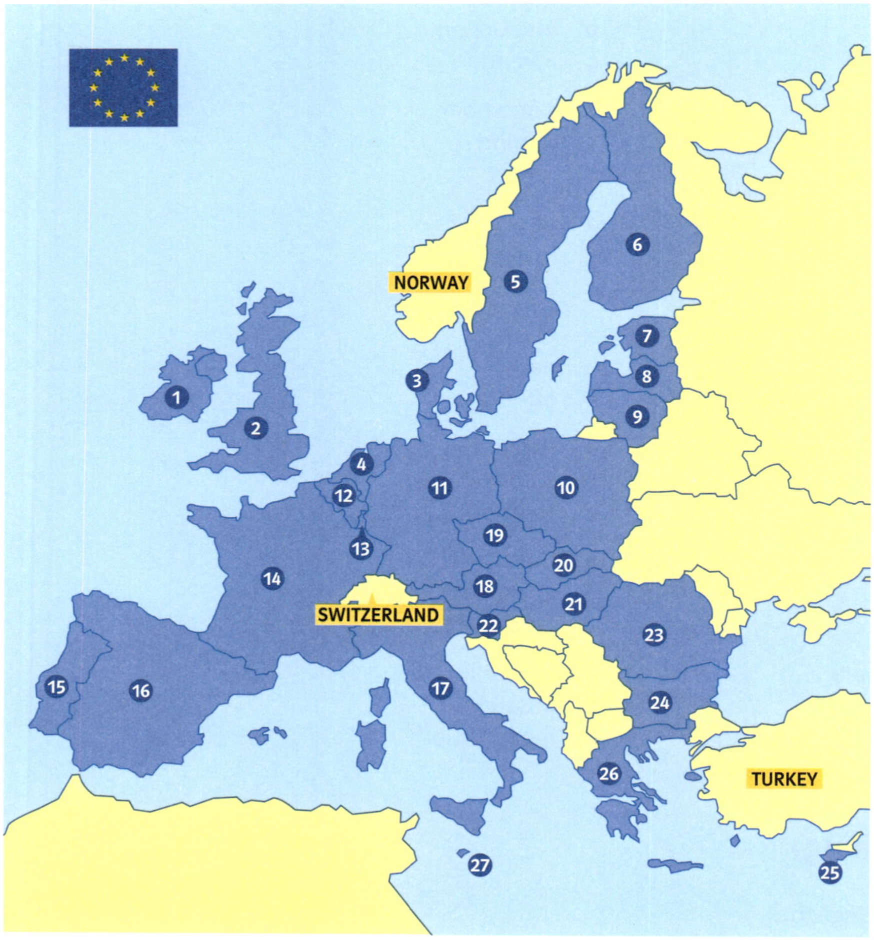

1. Ireland
2. ______
3. ______
4. ______
5. ______
6. ______
7. ______
8. ______
9. ______
10. ______
11. ______
12. ______
13. ______
14. ______
15. ______
16. ______
17. ______
18. ______
19. ______
20. ______
21. ______
22. ______
23. ______
24. ______
25. ______
26. ______
27. ______

Europe and the EU

The EU or European Union consists of *(besteht aus)* a total of **(1)** ______ countries. A small number of other countries are waiting to join. The most important of these is **(2)** ______. Three important European countries are not in the EU: Iceland, **(3)** ______ and **(4)** ______. The modern EU began in **(5)** 19______, but the first community of European countries was forty years earlier, in **(6)** ______. It was called the European Coal and Steel Community (ECSC) and its members were Germany, France, the Netherlands, Belgium, Luxembourg and Italy. The EU has many advantages for the people who live there. One is that it is much easier today than ever before to **(7)** ______ ***(reisen)*** and to **(8)** ______ ***(arbeiten)*** in another country. That means that people of different **(9)** ______ ***(Staatsangehörigkeiten)*** get to know each other better, too. A second advantage is that you can use the same money in many EU countries – the **(10)** ______. Those places where you can use this money are known as the **(11)** ______. Not all EU countries belong to this. One, of course, is **(12)** ______, where people still use the 'pound'.

B Language toolbox: Introducing yourself

1 **Henry, a Dutch student, is introducing himself at an international seminar. Find the headings below for the four speech bubbles *(Sprechblasen)*. Write in A, B, C or D.**

→ SB: S. 8–9, GS: A 1–2, A 5, A 8–12

☐ eine zeitlich begrenzte Handlung in der Gegenwart
☐ Handlungen in der Gegenwart, die auf Dauer gültig sind
☐ Zukunftspläne
☐ Ereignisse in der Vergangenheit

A Hi. My name's Henry van Etten. I live in Eindhoven in the Netherlands.

B I was born in Eindhoven and I went to school here. Last year, I started a 4-year course at an MBO, a *Middelbar Beroepsonderwijs* – you'd call that a vocational college.

C I'm training to be a furniture-maker.

D One day, I hope to design my own furniture and to have my own workshop, but first I'm going to work for a few years with a big manufacturer to get experience. I'd like to travel, too, maybe to Australia or the States.

2 **Sandra Kask is another vocational student at the seminar. Complete her introduction. Use the correct tenses and forms of the verbs in brackets (...).**

"Hello, I'm Sandra Kask and I (1) come (come) from Estonia. I (2) ________ (live) in the Estonian capital, Tallinn. I (3) ________ (not/be born) there, though. When I was very small, I (4) ________ (live) in a town called Valga, in the south of Estonia. My parents (5) ________ (move) to Tallinn from Valga when I (6) ________ (be) two years old. I (7) ________ (go) to my first school and my secondary school in Tallinn. I (8) ________ (leave) my secondary school last year and now I'm a student at a vocational college. I (9) ________ (study) office administration and English. It's a 30-month course and I (10) ________ (enjoy) it very much. After I finish, I (11) ________ (want) to travel. If possible, I (12) ________ (go/work) in the UK for a couple of years. I (13) ________ (visit) London two years ago and I (14) ________ (love) the city. Then I (15) ________ (plan) to return to Estonia. I (16) ________ (like) to work in a marketing company in Tallinn or maybe in the advertising industry."

3 **Anton Stempfhuber is from Germany. Finish this text about him with the simple present or present continuous forms of the verbs. REMEMBER! Some verbs are not normally used in the present continuous.**

Anton Stempfhuber (1) _is_ (be) from Saarbrücken in western Germany. He (2) ______ (be) 25 years old and he (3) ______ (work) as a chef in the kitchen of one of the city's best hotels. Anton (4) ______ (like) his job very much indeed. He (5) ______ (have) friendly colleagues and he (6) ______ (think) that the work is both creative and challenging. Right now, however, Anton (7) ______ (not/be) in Saarbrücken. He (8) ______ (do) a 6-month work placement with the EU Leonardo da Vinci programme. He (9) ______ (spend) the six months in a Michelin starred restaurant in Paris where he (10) ______ (train) under one of France's top chefs. "The experience (11) ______ (be) an absolute dream," says Anton. "I (12) ______ (learn) so much here. I (13) ______ (like) Paris, too. One day, I definitely (14) ______ (want) to work here full-time."

4 **Here's one more young European. Her name's Lucia Moreno. You meet her in your hometown in Germany and want to find out more about her. Look at Lucia's answers and complete your questions.**

You Where (1) _do you come_ from, Lucia?
Lucia I come from Segovia.
You Sorry, my geography's terrible. That's in Spain, right?
Lucia Right! It's in the centre of Spain.
You But you're in Germany right now. How long (2) ______?
Lucia I'm spending three months here. It's part of my college course.
You Oh, you're a college student. What course (3) ______?
Lucia I'm on a 2-year Travel and Tourism course.
You So when (4) ______?
Lucia I came here two weeks ago.
You And (5) ______?
Lucia Mmm, I don't know yet if I like the town or not. Everything is still very new and strange.

5 **Lucia has some questions for you, too. Continue your conversation with her. Write on a separate piece of paper. Begin like this:**

Lucia And what about you? Do you live here? I mean, you're German, right?

D Business topics

→ SB: S.12–13

1 Match the expressions and the definitions, then use them to complete the sentences below.

1 o	2	3	4	5	6	7	8
9	10	11	12	13	14	15	

1	war	a	Person who buys things.
2	unthinkable	b	Countries which trade together commercially.
3	democracy	c	Rule that the government makes.
4	standard of living	d	Able to travel and move around.
5	trading bloc	e	How a country organises its schools is its ~.
6	consumer	f	If you are ~ of something you are for (not against) it.
7	right (n.)	g	If you have the ~ to do something, you are allowed to do it.
8	mobile (adj.)	h	Impossible (to imagine).
9	law	i	Political system in which people choose their politicians.
10	environment	j	The amount of money and the quality of life that people have.
11	currency	k	Second possibility.
12	alternative	l	The group of politicians who make laws for a country.
13	in favour of	m	The money that people use in a country is its ~.
14	education system	n	The world around us.
15	parliament	o	When two or more countries fight together.

1. There's a __law__ which says that you can't smoke in restaurants.
2. Are you __________ of the EU? – No! I'm against it.
3. What __________ do they use in Norway? – I think it's the Krone.
4. Where does the European __________ sit? – Well, it sits for three weeks every month in Brussels, and for one week in Strasbourg.
5. People in countries like Germany and Great Britain have a much better __________ than people in African countries. They have more money, nicer houses, cars and so on.
6. The Second World __________ began in 1939 and ended in 1945.
7. We don't want to do this but I'm afraid there's no __________ .
8. I'm not going to do that. It's __________ !
9. People move around more nowadays. They're much more __________ than in the past.
10. In a __________ , people have the __________ to choose their politicans.

2 In exercise 1 above, *four* expressions have a definition but are not in the sentences 1–10. Which? Write them here:

a __________ b __________ c __________ d __________

Now write a sentence yourself with each expression.

a ____________________

b ____________________

c ____________________

d ____________________

3 EXTRA Nationality words. Look at the table and finish the sentences below.

→ SB: S.14–15

Erik Fischer is from **Germany**.
He's **German**. (Or: He's **a German**.)
He loved the food that he ate in **Britain**.
He loved **British** food.
He thought **the British** were friendly.

1 *-(i)an*

Country	Adjective	Person	Population (people)
Germany	German	a German	the Germans
Austria	Austrian	an Austrian	the Austrians

Also: **Belgium** (Belgian / a Belgian / the Belgians); **Bulgaria** (Bulgarian / a Bulgarian / the Bulgarians); **Estonia** (Estonian); **Hungary** (Hungarian); **Italy** (Italian); **Latvia** (Latvian); **Lithuania** (Lithuanian); **Romania** (Romanian); **Slovakia** (Slovakian); **Slovenia** (Slovenian)

2 Other nationalities

Britain	British	a British person*	the British
Cyprus	Cypriot	a Cypriot	the Cypriots
Czech Republic	Czech	a Czech	the Czechs
Denmark	Danish	a Dane	the Danes
Finland	Finnish	a Finn	the Finns
France	French	a Frenchwoman/man	the French
Greece	Greek	a Greek	the Greeks
Iceland	Icelandic	an Icelander	the Icelanders
Ireland	Irish	an Irishwoman/man	the Irish
Luxembourg	Luxembourgian	a Luxembourger	the Luxembourgers
Malta	Maltese	a Maltese	the Maltese
The Netherlands	Dutch	a Dutchwoman/man	the Dutch
Norway	Norwegian	a Norwegian	the Norwegians
Poland	Polish	a Pole	the Poles
Portugal	Portuguese	a Portuguese	the Portuguese
Spain	Spanish	a Spaniard	the Spanish
Sweden	Swedish	a Swede	the Swedes
Switzerland	Swiss	a Swiss	the Swiss
Turkey	Turkish	a Turk	the Turks

* *'a Briton' is sometimes used in newspapers. In everyday language people also sometimes say: 'a Brit/the Brits'.*

1. Sandra is from Finland. She's a Finn (or: She's Finnish).
2. Jan is from Poland. He's a ____________ (or: He's ____________).
3. I was in Portugal last week. ____________ food is delicious.
4. Belgium is famous for its chips. The ____________ have the best chips in Europe!
5. Norway isn't an EU country. The ____________ don't want to be part of the EU.
6. Eva is a young ____________ from Dublin in the Irish Republic.
7. The flags of Bulgaria, Italy and Hungary are all the same colour. The ____________, ____________ and ____________ flags are all red, white and green.
8. *Swatch* is a ____________ company that makes watches.
9. The movie actor Antonio Banderas is Italian, isn't he? – No! He's from Spain. He's a ____________.
10. *Glitnir* is the name of a bank in Iceland. It's the third largest ____________ bank.
11. The official currency of Turkey is the ____________ Lira (TL).

Video lounge

→ SB: S.15, Schüler DVD V1, Schüler DVD-Transkript

1 **Before you watch the video, look at the vocabulary in the box and complete the sentences.**

I was supposed (to do) *ich sollte (etwas tun)*
I changed my mind *ich habe es mir anders überlegt*
be within easy reach *leicht erreichbar sein*
decamp (to) *aufbrechen (nach)*
transition *Übergang*
baggage allowance *Freigepäck(menge)*
start from scratch *bei Null anfangen*
get it together *sein Leben in den Griff bekommen*
enrol *sich anmelden*
work on (doing sthg.) *dabei sein (etwas zu tun)*
Soho *Stadtteil Londons*
sign from God *Zeichen Gottes*
serve a purpose *einen Zweck erfüllen*
do some readjusting *sich neu einstellen*
pretty much *so ziemlich*
hang out (with s.o.) *(mit jmdm.) herumhängen*
there is something going on *es passiert etwas*

1. I was supposed to go to New York but I changed ________ and went to Washington DC.
2. When you fly, you are allowed to take 20kg of baggage. Your ________ is 20kg.
3. At the weekend, I often ________ my friends in town.
4. The sea is within ________ of the town and in summer everyone ________ to the beach.
5. The first thing I did when I arrived in London was to ________ at a language school.
6. They had nothing when they arrived in the new country. They had to ________ from ________.
7. However, they worked hard, made friends and slowly they got it ________.
8. There's a MacDonald's in ________ every city in the world now.
9. The ________ from being a student to having a job and working isn't always easy. People often have to do some ________.
10. Have you found an apprenticeship yet? – No, but I'm ________ it!
11. Life in modern Europe is really interesting. There's ________ exciting ________.

2 **Watch the video in sections and answer the questions. Write on a separate piece of paper.**

Section 1: In the U-Bahn and at the beach.

1. Where was Seema supposed to go? Why did she change her mind and go to Berlin?
2. What things are within easy reach of Berlin city centre? What happens in summer?
3. Who spent the first weekend in Berlin with Seema? What did that give her ('Which was nice')?
4. After that weekend she was 'starting completely from scratch again'. What *three* problems does she mention? How did she feel about that situation?
5. Then she says she 'slowly got it together'. What *four* things does she mention?

Section 2: On her bike in town. Tip: Seema sometimes speaks quickly in this section. Remember that you can also read the text of the video on your DVD to help you.

6. How did Seema start learning German? Where did she find the books?
7. Enrolling at the language school in Berlin 'served two purposes' for Seema. What are the two purposes?

Section 3: In Seema's flat.

8. Why did Seema's family have 'to do some readjusting in their head' at first? How did they feel later?
9. What does she say about Europe today? What should young people do in Seema's opinion?

3 **Listen one more time and check your answers. Then write a short text about Seema – 'A Brit in Berlin'.**

More listening practice in *Business Expert*
Remember that you can listen to many of the texts in your book. Look for the DVD sign: A1.1

2 A letter of application

1 **Read about this German student called Lorenzo Bauer. Then look at the advertisement and write notes in the grid below it in German.**

Lorenzo Bauer is a student at a vocational college in Bielefeld. He's in the second year of a two-year full-time Business and Administration course. He hopes to become a *Speditionskaufmann* – a management assistant in freight forwarding.

Before beginning work, Lorenzo would like to do a 6-month work placement in an English-speaking country and right now he's looking at an advertisement in a student magazine called IrelandLink. Lorenzo thinks that he'd like to apply for the placement.

Interested in a work placement in the Republic of Ireland?

Shannon Airport is Ireland's largest airport and one of Europe's fastest-growing, with around 4 million passengers last year. It is also the centre of the Republic's airfreight cargo business and is home to many of the world's major logistics companies including FedEx, DHL, TNT and UPS.

shannon AIRPORT
AERFORT NA sionainne

Internships (work placements)

The airport is pleased to offer internships to international students and we are currently looking for interns to work in our marketing and airfreight departments. Applicants must be aged between 18 and 25, and have excellent computer skills and a good knowledge of English. Internships are available for 3 or 6 months. Accommodation is available either with local Irish families or at an international student hostel 1 kilometer from the airport. Interns will receive a monthly wage of €450.

How to apply

If you are interested in a work placement with us, please write enclosing your current CV to:
Linda Kearney
Shannon Airport
County Clare, Ireland

Land/Stadt	(Republik) Irland/Shannon
Art des Unternehmens	
Art der Tätigkeit(en)	
Voraussetzungen	
Bezahlung	
Unterkunft	
Name der Kontaktperson	

2 Lorenzo wrote the letter of application below. In the box, there is some extra information about Lorenzo. Use it, the text about him on page 14 and the advertisement to complete the letter. Remember to use the correct layout for a formal personal letter.

Address: Walkenweg 17, 33605 Bielefeld, Germany
Work experience: completed a 4-week work placement last year in the freight forwarding department of a large German logistics company
Hobbies: football, hockey and ice skating

(1) ______________________
____
____

(2) ______________________
____
____
____

4 February 20 __

(3) ______________________

(4) ______________________

I would like to apply for one of the internships in your airfreight department which you advertised in the magazine (5) ______________ of 3 February.

I am currently in the second year of (6) ______________________ at a vocational college in (7) ______________, Germany. At the end of the course I will obtain my 'Fachhochschulreife' qualification. That is equivalent to a BTEC National Certificate in Ireland. I hope to become (8) ______________________.

As you will see from my enclosed CV, I have excellent computer skills and a good knowledge of English (B2 Level in the Common European Framework). As part of my college course last year, I successfully completed (9) ______________________.
I have a wide range of interests including (10) ______________________.

I would very much welcome the opportunity to work at Shannon Airport and believe that I would be a valuable and enthusiastic employee. I hope that you will consider my application and look forward to hearing from you.

(11) ______________________
Lorenzo Bauer
Lorenzo Bauer
(12) ______________________

3 Write in English phrases.

Nesrin Yüksel, a student in Cologne, is also applying for a work placement at the moment. The placement is for six months in a hotel in Canada and she saw the advertisement for it online.

Nesrin has made some notes in German about what she would like to say in her letter of application. Write in the English phrases that she can use.

1. Sehr geehrter Herr MacKenzie,
   Dear Mr MacKenzie
2. ich möchte mich auf die auf der Canada Tourism Website ausgeschriebene Praktikumsstelle bewerben.
3. Zurzeit bin ich im zweiten Jahr eines zweijährigen Kurses an einer berufsbildenden Schule in Köln, Deutschland.
4. Wie aus meinem Lebenslauf zu ersehen ist, verfüge ich über gute Englisch- und Computerkenntnisse.
5. Ich bin fleißig, lernwillig und ein kommunikativer Mensch.
6. Ich verfüge bereits über Berufserfahrung im Hotelwesen *(in the hotel industry)*. Letztes Jahr habe ich in meinen Sommerferien in einem internationalen Hotel in der Türkei gearbeitet.
7. In meiner Freizeit interessiere ich mich u.a. für Sport, Musik und Tanzen.
8. Über die Möglichkeit, in einem kanadischen Hotel zu arbeiten, würde ich mich sehr freuen.
9. Ich hoffe, dass Sie meine Bewerbung in Betracht ziehen, und freue mich auf Ihre Antwort.
10. Mit freundlichen Grüßen,

4 Now YOU.

- **Read the advertisement below. Copy the grid on page 14 and complete it in German about the placements.**
- **Write an email to apply for a placement. Give your own details and use today's date.**
- EXTRA **Attach your current CV.**

praktikumsbörse.de → Praktika im Ausland → Australien

Work placements with the Australian Broadcasting Corporation, Sydney

The Australian Broadcasting Corporation (ABC) is Australia's national radio and television provider. ABC Commercial is the division of the corporation which markets and sells ABC products – such as its most popular TV shows – worldwide. ABC Commercial is currently offering work placements in its international marketing department. Placements are available from a minimum of 6 months to a maximum of 12 months and applicants – who must be aged between 18 and 30 – should be free to take up their placement in July this year. No previous experience of TV or radio work is necessary, but applicants should have a basic knowledge of marketing and general office administration.

A good knowledge of English and good internet and computer skills are both essential. Australia is a dynamic, open and friendly country and we are looking particularly for young people who work well in a team, are good communicators, and have plenty of energy and enthusiasm. ABC Commercial cannot pay applicants' travel costs to and from Australia, but we are pleased to offer free accommodation during the placement in a local student hostel. Furthermore, ABC Commercial will pay a monthly salary of AU$800. Interns will also benefit from 30 days' paid holiday.

To apply, email julie.cameron@abc_commercial.au attaching your current CV.

5 ROUNDUP **Here are some of the keywords from Unit 2. Use them to complete the sentences.**

a good communicator • a good knowledge of English • advertised • advertisement • applicant • wage • application • currently • hard working • internship • keen to learn • reliable • to apply • unpaid

1. When you want to apply for a job or a work placement, you write a letter of ______.
2. A person who applies for a job is an ______.
3. Another word for a work placement is an ______.
4. People often find out about jobs or work placements when they see an ______ online or in a newspaper.
5. Letters often begin with the words: 'I would like to apply for the work placement which you ______ on the Praktikumsbörse website'.
6. Another word for 'at the moment' is ______.
7. Employers often say that they are looking for people who are ______, ______, ______ and ______.
8. ______ is also often essential.
9. Some work placements are ______ *(unbezahlt)*, but sometimes people also receive a ______.

3 Managing basic business situations (1)

A Young experts talking

→ SB: S. 24–25

1 **These are the offices of Falke GmbH. It's a world-leading manufacturer of bicycle tyres *(Reifen)*. Read about the buildings then complete the sentences with the names of the departments and other important places.**

Falke's offices are in two parts. To the right of the main entrance is Building A. It is three floors high. To the left is Building B. It has four floors. The top floor is an 'archive' where the company keeps all its important documents.

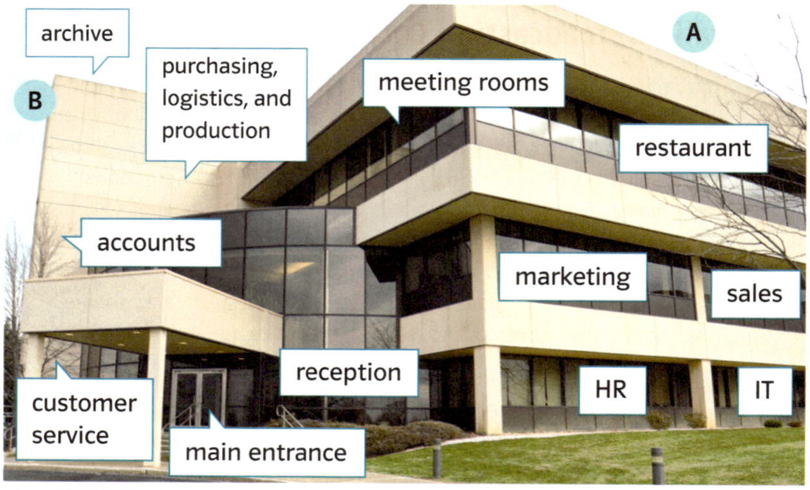

1. Employees and visitors enter here. main entrance
2. It's on the second floor in Building A. Employees eat here at lunchtime. ______
3. This department in Building B deals with customers' problems. ______
4. Falke keeps important documents here, usually for six years. ______
5. People from Falke often welcome their visitors here. ______
6. These rooms are important when clients visit. ______
7. This department looks after the company's money. ______
8. These three departments, all on the second floor in Building B, organise production, buy raw materials and distribute Falke's products. (a) ______ (b) ______ (c) ______
9. These two departments are next to each other in Building A. One advertises Falke's products, the second sells them. (a) ______ (b) ______
10. On the ground floor *(Erdgeschoss)*, below those two departments, are the departments which look after the computer network and recruit and train employees. (a) ______ (b) ______

2 **You use an *ing*-form after lots of expressions that end with a preposition. One is *be responsible for*. Write sentences about these other departments.**

→ GS: D6 (7)

1. The sales department is responsible for selling Falke's products.
2. The accounts department ______.
3. The purchasing department ______.
4. The IT department ______.
5. The logistics department ______.
6. The customer service department ______.

B Language toolbox: Describing companies

→ SB: S. 26–27, GS: H1, H2

1 **Ivan Shironosov – on the left in the picture – is a management assistant at Falke. He's welcoming a visitor. Complete the text with *who, which* or *that*. (Tip: In all the sentences, *who, which* and *that* are the subject).**

Ivan is a management assistant in wholesale and foreign trade at Falke GmbH, an important German company **(1)** which makes bicycle tyres. The person **(2)** ____________ is visiting Falke's offices today is Bob Corff. Bob is from Fat Dog Bikes, an American firm **(3)** ____________ manufactures and sells bikes across the USA. After welcoming Bob, Ivan will take him up to one of the meeting rooms **(4)** ____________ are on the second floor. Here, Bob will meet Martin Rössle, Ivan's boss and the manager **(5)** ____________ is in charge of sales to North America.

2 **In each pair of sentences below, the relative pronoun *(who, which, that)* is the subject in one sentence but the object in the other. Which is which? Write in S (= subject) or O (= object).**

1a. Herr Rössle is the man who is in charge of sales to the USA. [S]
1b. The man that Ivan is meeting is called Bob Corff. [ ]
2a. Falke is a company which makes bicycle tyres. [ ]
2b. The tyres which it makes are famous worldwide. [ ]
3a. Cycling enthusiasts in the USA love the bikes that Fat Dog makes. [ ]
3b. Fat Dog makes bikes which are ideal for mountain trails. [ ]
4a. Ivan likes the job that he has very much. [ ]
4b. He has a job which is fascinating. [ ]

What is the easy rule that helps you to see the difference between *who, which* and *that* as subject and object? Write it here (in German or English).

____

____

3 **In this text there are *four* sentences where *who, which* or *that* is the object. Underline the sentences and write them again below as 'contact clauses'.**

The building that you can see on page 18 is the headquarters of Falke GmbH. Visitors who arrive there enter through the main entrance and there is usually someone from Falke who meets and welcomes them. One reason why Ivan likes his job so much is because he meets lots of Americans and Canadians. He enjoys speaking English with the people that he meets. And he has the chance to travel with his boss, too. He likes seeing the places that he visits. He has visited many different companies which buy Falke's products. So he has been to New York, Chicago, Seattle and Toronto. The city which he liked best was Seattle.

1. ____

2. ____

3. ____

4. ____

4 At the start of the meeting, Ivan's boss Herr Rössle would like Ivan to describe Falke to Bob Corff. Ivan has made some notes in German. Write a short text in English that Ivan can use. Write on a separate piece of paper. Begin like this.

Welcome again to Falke, Mr Corff. I'd like to tell you first a little bit about our company …

- größter Hersteller von Fahrradreifen in Deutschland
- weltweit tätig
- Verkaufsbüros in 24 Ländern
- mit Sitz in Deutschland
- Zentrale hier in Remagen
- F&E Abteilung in Bonn, Deutschland
- Produktionsanlagen in Korea (Korea) und Litauen
- 1923 gegründet
- Unternehmensgründer: Willi und Albrecht Kaiser (Brüder)
- noch immer in Familienbesitz
- gegenwärtige Inhaberin: Großenkelin (great-granddaughter) von Albrecht Kaiser

D Business topics

→ SB: S. 30–31

1 On page 21 is some more information about Fat Dog Bikes from its website. Read the web page and write notes in English into the mindmap below.

FAT DOG BIKES

Business
(What kind of company? Product(s)?)
- manufacturer
- cycles, cycling accessories

Interesting fact?

Founded
(When? By?)

Turnover
(How much does it earn?)

Operations
(Where does it sell its products? How? And in the future?)

Employees
(How many people work for the company?)

Headquarters
(Where is it based?)

About us

Headquartered in Janesville, Wisconsin, the Fat Dog Bicycle Corporation is the fifth largest American manufacturer of bicycles with a turnover last year of $607 million. Our product range includes town bicycles, road racing cycles, and cycling accessories, but our flagship product is the Mountain Ace 800, a cutting-edge bicycle designed for mountain trails. Founded in 1976 by Steve Beglinger and Elizabeth Prosnick, Fat Dog's first workshop was a barn on Elizabeth's father's farm. Back in those early days, there were just five employees; now there are 1,500–850 of them in our factory in Janesville. Because here at Fat Dog we love cycles ourselves, we understand the passion others have for them. We sell our products only through specialist dealers, many of them smaller bicycles stores. Our products are on sale in all 50 American States and since 2008 also through six dealers in Canada. We are currently planning to start selling our cycles in Europe – so watch out for more news!

FAT DOG BIKES
Two wheels.
One world.

Home | About us | Shop online | Newsletter | Investors | Careers

2 **Ivan's boss Herr Rössle wants information about Fat Dog Bikes. You are Ivan. Translate the text on the webpage into German. Use your dictionary if necessary.**

3 EXTRA **The history of a company. Here are some facts about Falke and Fat Dog. Write the years, numbers etc. again in words.**

→ SB: S. 32–33

1. Falke is Germany's leading bicycle tyre manufacturer. Fat Dog is the 5th fifth biggest cycle manufacturer in the U.S.
2. Falke was founded in 1923 ______________________,
   Fat Dog in 1976 ______________________.
3. Falke opened its factory in Korea in 2002 ______________________
   ______________________.
4. By 2012 ______________________,
   Fat Dog plans to have around 50 dealers in Europe.
5. Over ⅔ ______________________ of Fat Dog Bikes are mountain bikes.
6. Around ½ ______________________ of Falke's sales offices are in Europe.
7. Falke's turnover last year was €1.2 billion ______________________
   ______________________.
8. Last year the company spent €2.76 million ______________________
   ______________________ on research.
9. Fat Dog Bikes began in a barn on Elizabeth Prosnick's father's farm. The Prosnick family came to the USA in 1903 ______________________
   ______________________.
10. The Kaiser family (Willi and Albrecht founded Falke) came to Germany in 1883 ______________________.

Saying years

- You say most years before 2000 as two numbers:
  1937 nineteen / thirty-seven
- Years before 2000 that end in 01, 02, 03, … you can say with *oh* or *hundred and*:
  1901 nineteen oh one
  nineteen hundred and one
- You say years from 2000–2009 with *two thousand and:*
  2005 two thousand and five
- From 2010 most people now say years as two numbers with *twenty*:
  2010 twenty / ten
  2015 twenty / fifteen

Saying numbers

- Decimals: You use 'point' (not 'comma') in English:
  1.64 one point six four
- **billion** = Milliarde (1000 million)!
- Fractions: *(a) half, a quarter (¼), three quarters (¾), a third (⅓), three eighths (⅜)*
- It's the **fifth biggest** company = fünftgrößte

Video lounge

→ SB: S. 33, Schüler DVD V2, Schüler DVD-Transkript

1 **Before you watch the video, look at the vocabulary in the box and complete the sentences. You don't need all the expressions for the sentences.**

compare sthg. with sthg. *etw. mit etw. vergleichen*	**brave** (false friend!) *mutig*
I'm a great believer in *Ich bin grundsätzlich für*	**brilliant** *genial, hervorragend*
look over your shoulder *(mit Angst) zurückblicken*	**perform** *funktionieren, Leistung bringen*
be immersed in *in etw. vertieft sein*	**bring out (a product)** *auf den Markt bringen*
gimmick *(technische) Spielerei*	**for its own sake** *um ihrer selbst willen*
gimmicky *effekthascherisch*	**create** *schaffen*
see through sthg. *(einen Trick) durchschauen*	**I reckon that** *ich glaube / meine, dass*
label sthg. *etw. als … bezeichnen*	**adjust** *sich (auf eine neue Situation) einstellen*
advertising *Werbung*	**the key thing** *die Hauptsache*
on the basis that *weil*	**brand** *Marke*

1. If you compare our products with their products, our products are much better!
2. When did they ______ out their 800 Model? – In 2005.
3. The product looks great but it doesn't work. It's just a ______ .
4. People don't like gimmicky products. I think they ______ ______ them very quickly.
5. I'm a ______ in working hard. I think it's the only way to be successful.
6. Most people buy things on ______ they are good value for money *(preiswert)*.
7. Everyone can make a mistake. The ______ is to learn from your mistakes.
8. Tim works about 12 hours a day. He's totally ______ in his work.
9. Anja is always afraid that someone will criticise her. At work, she looks ______ ______ all the time.
10. I ______ that when I make decisions I'm wrong about 50 per cent of the time!

2 **Watch the video in sections and answer the questions. Write on a separate piece of paper.**

Section 1: Introduction
James Dyson begins like this. Finish the sentence. "I'm afraid there aren't any rules, except probably one little rule I do have actually is that when you react to a situation, you should probably think what you should do and then what you shouldn't, and …

Section 2: James Dyson founded his company in 1991 …
When he started his business, Mr Dyson "looked around at vacuum cleaners." What did he decide about them? How did that compare with some other products? Explain.

Section 3: Dyson made over a thousand prototypes …
James Dyson is famous because he made over 1,000 prototypes before he finally built his first vacuum cleaner and then he sold vacuum cleaners only for 18 years. What does he say in his interview about this? Was he happy or not happy about that situation? Why (not)?

Section 4: For the last eight years Dyson has been the UK's top selling vacuum cleaner …
What does Mr Dyson say about (a) gimmicks, (b) advertising his new product?

Section 5: The ethos
True or false? 'The most important thing for Mr Dyson is making money'. Explain.

Section 6: Mistakes
True or false? 'Mr Dyson thinks that you should worry about your mistakes'. Explain.

Section 7: Obsession
What is the 'key thing' for Mr Dyson? Why?

3 **What do YOU think about Mr Dyson? Is he a 'typical' businessman? What are his most important business ideas in your opinion?**

4 The language of emailing

1 **Write the email addresses.**

1. Mike dot Harris at Google dot com — mike.harris@google.com
2. L dot Williams at BT hyphen Online dot [ko] dot U-K
3. Ina dot Krüger at Web dot D-E
4. Liv dot Wagner at Nordfracht underscore sales dot D-E
5. Bodo hyphen Richter at Köln underscore net dot D-E

2 **Be polite. Look at the examples then write the sentences below again with *would* or *could*.**

***Would / Could you* + noun**

Would you (please)	send me	your latest sales figures?
Could you (please)	email me	the dates of the next meeting?
	let me have	the address of a good hotel?

***Would / Could you* + *when / where / if* (= ob)**

Would you (please)	tell me	when	you will be in Germany?
Could you (please)	let me know	where	the meeting will be?
		if	Mr Smith is in the office today?

1. Send me the dates of the trade fair next month.
   Would you please send me the dates of the trade fair next month?
2. Email me the name of your new sales manager.
3. Let me have the telephone number of your logistics company.
4. When will send your report *(Bericht)*?
   Could you tell me / let me know when you will send your report?
5. Where are your sales offices in the Netherlands?
6. Do you have Ms Jones's mobile number?
7. Email me the dates when your office will be closed.
8. Will someone meet me at the airport?
9. Where is your new factory?
10. Let us have your decision asap.

3 **Read the emails and answer the questions below in English. You can use notes.**

SITUATION
You work for the German chocolate manufacturer Milkoo. Milkoo chocolate is a household name *(allgemein bekannter Begriff)* in Germany, Austria and Switzerland. It also has good sales in the Netherlands and the UK. And it is very popular in Brazil, where you have a manufacturing facility. Milkoo's headquarters are near Munich. You are a management assistant in the sales department. Your boss is Ann-Katrin Dabbert. This morning, you have these emails in your inbox *(Posteingang)*.

Von: rafael.costa@milkoo.br
Gesendet: 24. Oktober 20 _ _ 15:29
An: your name@milkoo.de
Betreff: AW: trade fair in rio de janeiro
Anhang: Trade_Fair.doc (105 KB)

Dear *(Your name)*
Thanks for your email. You asked about the trade fair in Rio de Janeiro next month. In the attachment you'll find full details of dates etc. Please let me know if I can help further.
Kind regards
Rafael

Von: melissa.taylor@milkoo.co.uk
Gesendet: 24. Oktober 20 _ _ 17.15
An: your name@milkoo.de
Betreff: product launch

Dear *(Your name)*
We're all very excited here in the London office about the launch in January of the new Milkoo Strawberry Bar. Could you let us have any sales literature asap so that we can translate it into English? Thanks in advance!
All the best
Melissa

Von: melissa.taylor@milkoo.co.uk
Gesendet: 24. Oktober 20 _ _ 17.18
An: your name@milkoo.de
Betreff: Ms Dabbert's next visit

Dear *(Your name)*
Me again! Sorry, I forgot to ask something in my last email. Could you also send us the dates of Ms Dabbert's next visit to the UK and let me know if you would like me to arrange hotels, a hire car etc.?

All the best
Melissa

Von: wim.de_vries@milkoo.nl
Gesendet: 24. Oktober 20 _ _ 18.04
An: your name@milkoo.de
Betreff: office reorganisation

Hi *(Your name)*
Hope all's well with you in Germany. This is to let you know that the Amsterdam office will be closed for two days next month (28 and 29 November) while we reorganise and install a new computer network. Sounds great fun ☹
Best wishes
Wim de Vries

► **product launch** *Produkteinführung* ► **sales literature** *Verkaufsprospekte* ► **hire car** *Mietwagen*

1. Who is asking you for information, documents etc.? What do they want?

____

____

2. Who is giving you information? What is the information?

____

____

4 You talk to your boss, Frau Dabbert, and make notes about how to reply to the four emails. Write the emails. Use your dictionary if necessary. The first one is partly done for you.

Rafael
- Danke für die Infos über die Messe.
- Bitte senden Sie uns eine Liste von guten Hotels in Rio. Danke im Voraus!

Melissa (E-Mail 1)
- Danke für die E-Mail. Wir freuen uns auch über die Produkteinführung. Verkaufsprospekte werden am 15. November erhältlich sein. Wir werden sie sofort per Post versenden (we'll send).

Melissa (E-Mail 2)
- In der Anlage finden Sie die Details zu Frau Dabberts nächstem Besuch.
- Hotels können wir hier buchen, aber bitte einen Mietwagen vom 4.-8. Dez. besorgen. Danke!

Wim
- Danke für die Infos.
- Bitte sagen Sie uns Bescheid, ob wir Sie am 28. und 29. Nov. per Telefon erreichen können. Haben Sie auch eine Mobilnummer?
- Bitte schicken Sie uns bis (by) 27. Nov. Ihre monatlichen Absatzzahlen für November.
- Viel Glück beim Umzug!

An: rafael.costa@milkoo.br
Kopie an: a-k.dabbert@milkoo.de
Betreff: AW AW trade fair in rio de janeiro

Dear Rafael

Thanks very much for the information about **(1)** ______________________ ______________________ You asked very kindly if you could help further. Yes please! **(2)** ______________________ ______________________ us a list of good hotel in Rio? Thanks **(3)** ______________ !

Best regards

(Your name)

5 **ROUNDUP** **Each email phrase has a missing word. What is it?**

1. Thanks _in_ advance!
2. In the ______________ you'll find …
3. Could you please ______________ me know …
4. Looking ______________ to hearing from you soon.
5. You ______________ to know …
6. You ______________ about …
7. Please let me know if you have any ______________ ______________ questions.
8. I'm ______________ I haven't replied before.
9. I'm ______________ I don't have the information you asked about.
10. I'm sorry you couldn't ______________ the file.
11. How are ______________ going?
12. ______________, thanks.
13. I'm ______________ the document you asked for.
14. ______________ you please tell me … ?

5 Managing basic business situations (2)

A Young experts talking

→ SB: S. 42–43

1 **Silvia Scholz is a management assistant at a regional newspaper in North Rhine-Westphalia. Match the verbs 1–10 and the expressions a–j then complete the sentences about things Silvia does in her job. Use the same expressions as on page 43 of your book.**

1	book	**a**	a flight
2	have	**b**	a hotel room
3	listen to	**c**	a meeting
4	look after	**d**	a problem
5	make	**e**	lunch
6	reserve	**f**	notes (during a meeting)
7	sit in on	**g**	the minutes of a meeting
8	solve	**h**	travel arrangements
9	take	**i**	voicemail messages
10	write up	**j**	your boss's diary

1 a		**2**	
3		**4**	
5		**6**	
7		**8**	
9		**10**	

1. She looks after her boss's diary.
2. Her boss has a team meeting every Monday. Silvia always ______ ______ the meetings and ______ notes.
3. Afterwards, she ______ the minutes.
4. Silvia's boss frequently goes on business trips. Silvia always ______ ______ the travel arrangements for these trips.
5. For example, she often ______ flights and ______ ______ hotel rooms.
6. Silvia's first task in the morning is the same every day. She always ______ the voicemail messages on her answerphone.
7. Silvia usually ______ lunch with two friends in the company restaurant.

always, often etc.

You often use these with verbs in the **simple present**.

REMEMBER: *always, often* etc. go **before** a main verb (Hauptverb):
I *often* write letters.
(NOT! ~~I write often~~ letters.)

→ GS: A1, 3

2 **Silvia is talking on the phone to a British businessman. He wants to speak to Silvia's boss, Kris Holweg. Finish the conversation with the correct English phrases.**

Silvia Rheinische Allgemeine Zeitung. Scholz.
Caller Oh, hi. Do you speak English, please?
Silvia **(1)** ______ *(Sicher)*. I'm Silvia Scholz. How may I help you?
Caller **(2)** ______ *(Ich hätte gern mit … gesprochen)* Mr Holweg, please?
Silvia **(3)** ______ *(Wer ist am Apparat)*, please?
Caller **(4)** ______ *(Hier spricht)* Trevor Graham from the Oxford Times, in England.
Silvia **(5)** ______ *(Würden Sie Ihren Namen bitte buchstabieren?)*
Caller Graham. G-R-A-H-A-M. My first name is Trevor. T-R-E-V-O-R.
Silvia Thanks, Mr Graham. **(6)** ______ ______ *(Moment, bitte. Ich verbinde.)*

B Language toolbox: arrangements

→ SB: S. 44–45, GS: A10–12

1 **Match these verbs and expressions.**

1	discuss	a	a meeting (with somebody)
2	go to (or attend)	b	a place *(×2)*
3	have	c	a presentation
4	interview	d	a problem / a project / plans etc.
5	make (or give)	e	a trade fair / a conference
6	return from	f	an applicant
7	travel to		

1 d 2 3
4 5
6 7

2 **What's Mr Holweg doing next week? First, fill in the missing words, then answer the questions about his diary.**

On Monday morning ______ 9.30, he's …

______ Tuesday afternoon ______ 3.15 he's …

______ the morning he's … and ______ the afternoon / evening he's …

← Previous	Week 14 May – 20 May	Next →
Day	**am**	**pm**
Monday 14	9.30: Meeting with marketing team	2.00: Interview applicants for IT technician's job
Tuesday 15	11.00: Brunch with Steffen and Jakob from image22 (RAZ's advertising agency)	3.15: Meeting with Katja Wingartz (RAZ accounts dept.) to discuss budgets
Wednesday 16	Prepare presentation (see Sat)	Visit RAZ's printing works
Thursday 17	All day: work at home	
Friday 18	9.00: Meeting with sales manager	15.14: Travel to Amsterdam
Saturday 19 **(Sunday 20)**	Conference (Amsterdam): *Newspapers and the internet*	2.45: Make presentation 5.34: Return to Dusseldorf

► *RAZ (Rheinische Allgemeine Zeitung)* ► **advertising agency** *Werbeagentur* ► **printing works** *Druckerei*

1. What's he doing on Monday and Tuesday next week?
   On Monday morning at

2. What's he doing on Wednesday?

3. What about Thursday? Is he coming into the office? (What's he doing?)

4. What's he doing and at what times on Friday?

5. What's he doing on Saturday afternoon and evening?

3 **Here are the details of Mr Holweg's journeys next week and of the conference in Amsterdam. Answer the questions again.**

TRAIN TIMETABLE			
Outward journey	**Depart**	**Arrive**	**Duration**
Dusseldorf-Amsterdam	15.14	17.25	2 hrs 11 mins
Return journey	**Depart**	**Arrive**	**Duration**
Amsterdam-Dusseldorf	17.34	19.46	2 hrs 12 mins

CONFERENCE TIMETABLE	
Fri 18 May **8.00 pm**	Reception and Welcome
Sat 19 May **9.00 am**	Presentations and discussions
1.00 pm	Lunch
2.00 pm	Presentations and discussions
4.00 pm	End

duration *Dauer*
How long does ... take?
Wie lange dauert ...?

1. When does the conference begin?
H
2. When does it end?
3. When does Mr Holweg's train leave Dusseldorf on Friday afternoon?
4. How long does the journey to Amsterdam take?
5. When does he leave Amsterdam on Saturday and at what time does he arrive back in Dusseldorf?

4 **Because Mr Holweg is giving a presentation at the conference, the organisers want details of his travel arrangements in case *(falls)* they need to contact him. Write an email to the contact person, Marianne de Groot, with the following information:**

- *Fährt mit dem Zug nach Amsterdam. Kommt am Freitag, 18.05. um 17.25 an.*
- *Übernachtet am Amsterdam Hilton Tel: +31-20-710 60 00, Fax: +31-20-710 60 80*
- *Rückfahrt am 19.05. um 17.34.*
- *Bitte Bescheid sagen, wenn Sie weitere Informationen benötigen.*

An: m.de_groot@conferentie.nl
Kopie an: k.holweg@raz-marketing.de
Betreff:

Dear Ms de Groot

Thank you for your email. You asked about Mr Holweg's travel arrangements for the conference in Amsterdam. He will be travelling

D Business topics

→ SB: S. 48 – 49

1 Try this hotels crossword.

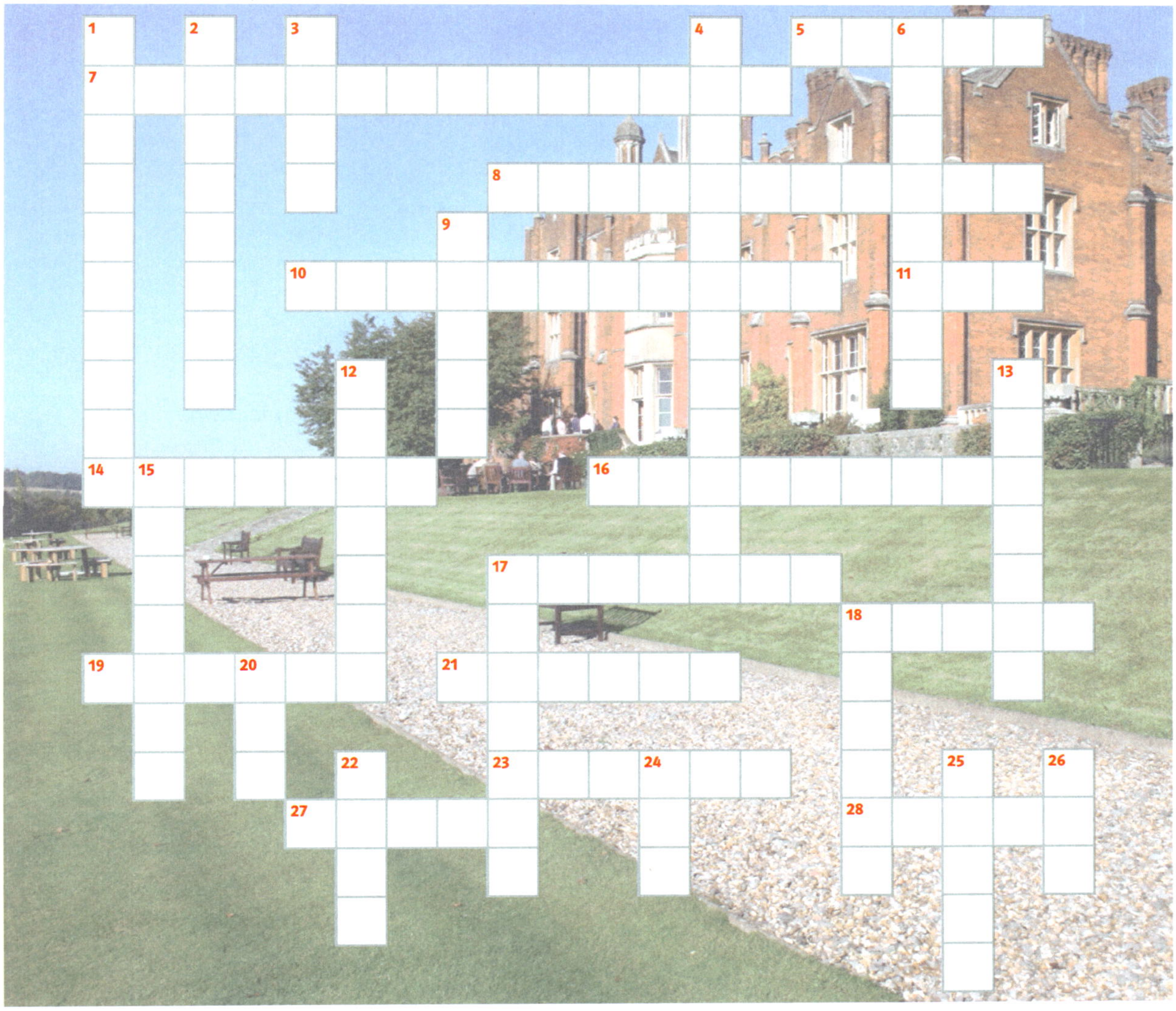

DOWN

1 The services etc. a hotel offers: restaurant, parking, free newspaper etc.
2 When the hotel staff smile, help you a lot, remember your name etc. they're being …
3 Reserve (a room).
4 Usually the first person you see at a hotel.
6 The room is … with TV and modem.
9 The best hotels have four or five, the cheapest one or two.
12 Does the price … breakfast? – No, that's extra.
13 I'm flying tomorrow. I need a hotel near the …
15 A room with a bathroom. An … bathroom.
17 The hotel washes your clothes. It has a … service.
18 Your room has internet …
20 You keep fit here.
22 The hotel is only five minutes' … *(zu Fuß)* from the station.
24 You eat in a restaurant and drink in a …
25 The opposite of a noisy hotel is a … hotel.
26 You can send documents with a … machine.

ACROSS

5 A person who stays at a hotel.
7 When it's 35° outside, you'll be glad your room is … *(two words)*
8 There are secretaries at the hotel to help you. The hotel offers a … service.
10 Not a full British breakfast, a … breakfast.
11 The price is £100 … night.
14 If you are hungry in your room, call room …
16 You can use this after washing your hair.
17 Situated.
18 A clock that wakes you up is an … clock.
19 A room for one person is a … room.
21 The bedrooms are *extremely* nice! They aren't just normal rooms, they're … rooms.
23 A room for two people is a … room.
27 There's a coffee … in your room so you can drink coffee whenever you want.
28 It's *very* hot there – but it's a good place to relax.

2 Silvia Scholz is talking on the phone to another caller who wants to speak to her boss, Mr Holweg. First write the British and American telephone numbers in words, then complete Silvia's conversation with the English telephone phrases.

→ SB: S. 50

British telephone numbers	American telephone numbers
1. 01286-225844: oh one two eight six, ______	**1.** 417-299 0808: ______
2. 020-4539 800: ______	**2.** 212-201 9962: ______

Silvia Rheinische Allgemeine Zeitung. Scholz.
Caller Good morning. Could I speak to Kris Holweg, please?
Silvia (1) I'm afraid he's in a meeting right now *(Tut mir leid, er ist momentan in einer Besprechung).* (2) ______ *(Darf er Sie in etwa einer halben Stunde zurückrufen?)*
Caller OK. (3) ______ *(Hier spricht)* Alison Bell from the Financial Times in London.
Silvia (4) ______ *(Hat Kris Ihre Telefonnummer, Frau Bell?)*
Caller I think so but (5) ______ *(ich gebe sie Ihnen nochmals).* It's 0044-20-511 6060.
Silvia (6) ______ *(Ich wiederhole).* 0044-20-511 6060.
Caller Right.
Silvia OK, (7) ______ *(ich sage Kris Bescheid, sobald er aus der Besprechung zurück ist.)*
Caller Thanks a lot.
Silvia (8) ______ *(Nichts zu danken),* Ms Bell. Bye now.

E Be an English expert!

→ SB: S. 50 (word families)

1 **Complete the sentences with a suitable word. It can be a noun, a verb or an adjective.**

1. We need to check that there's a room available. Could you phone and ask about availability?
2. Management assistants often have to ______ problems – find solutions to them, that is.
3. The agency sent us a really bad translation. Could you ______ this again, please?
4. Comfort is important when you stay at a hotel. The rooms have to be ______ .
5. My boss is flying to Scandinavia on Monday. His ______ is at 6 am.
6. The hotel has a superb location. It's ______ two minutes from the airport.
7. Would you make all the ______ for the trip, please, Sven? – Sure, I'll arrange it straight away.
8. Dick likes to stay fit. He always chooses hotels that have a ______ studio.
9. We have to think about the ______ of the trip. It can't be too expensive.

NOW YOU! **Write a second sentence below as in the examples above.**

10. We discussed the problem for over three hours!

______

6 A letter of enquiry

SITUATION
You work for TIEFHOCH, one of Germany's leading construction companies *(Baufirmen)*. It is based in Essen but operates worldwide. You are an industrial management assistant in the purchasing department at TIEFHOCH's headquarters. Your boss, Mr Nils Clemens, is one of the company's purchasing managers.

1 **Mr Clemens is always on the lookout for *(die Augen offen halten nach)* good new suppliers. You find this advertisement in a European trade magazine. Make notes about the advertisement for your boss in German in the table below. Use your dictionary if you need to.**

Ro Acoustic Insulation Systems from Norway

With over forty years' experience in the acoustic insulation industry, *Ro AS* ('ro' in Norwegian means 'peace', 'quiet') is today Norway's number one producer of acoustic insulation materials. Because of our leading position in the Scandinavian market, we are able to offer *exceptional* products at *exceptional* prices. In independent tests*, *Ro* acoustic insulation materials were found to be between 10 and 20% more efficient than those of major competitors. Our highly-trained team of technicians is also able to offer a full back-up service with advice and technical help.

Want to know more?
Visit our website: www.ro.com
Email: info@ro.com
Or write to us at: Ro AS, N-6146 Aheim, Norway

* EU Industry Standards Laboratory, Cerne, Switzerland, 2009

Our products

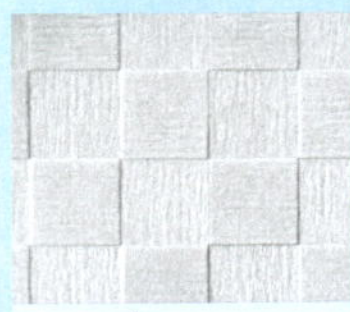
panels

foam

Over the years, *Ro* has developed a comprehensive range of products for the insulation of walls, ceilings and floors, both in private houses and in public buildings such as schools, offices, leisure complexes and cinemas.

Unternehmen	
Produkte / Anwendungen	
Weitere Dienstleistungen	
Kontakt	

2 **The parts of a letter of enquiry are usually in the same order. First, put the parts below in the correct order – write 1, 2, 3, . . . in the boxes. Then copy the letter of enquiry phrases a–i into the correct places in the table.**

- **a** Could you please send us your current sales brochure?
- **b** Our company is a rapidly growing retail business.
- **c** We would also be interested to learn about possible discounts and your delivery times.
- **d** We saw your products on your website
- **e** ~~We are currently looking for a new supplier.~~
- **f** We look forward to hearing from you in the near future.
- **g** We were interested in your advertisement in the European Industry Journal of 24 August.
- **h** You can find more information about us on our website.
- **i** We are a major German manufacturer of electrical equipment *(Elektrogeräte)*

☐ **Why you are writing and what you would like**

1. We are currently looking for a new supplier.

2. ______

3. ______

☐ 1 **Where you found out about a supplier**

4. ______

5. ______

______

☐ **Ending your letter**

6. ______

☐ **Your company**

7. ______

8. ______

9. ______

3 **Each sentence below has a missing phrase. Complete the sentences.**

1. You were recommended to us by one of our customers.
(Sie sind uns von einem Kunden empfohlen worden.)

2. We are a ______ .
(Wir sind ein führendes deutsches Unternehmen.)

3. ______ , we may buy large quantities of your products.
(Sollten Ihre Preise konkurrenzfähig sein, werden wir möglicherweise große Mengen Ihrer Produkte kaufen.)

4. Please let us know about ______ .
(Wir bitten um Angaben zu möglichen Rabatten.)

5. We would like to receive ______ of your products ______ .
(Wir würden gern zum Testen Muster Ihrer Produkte erhalten.)

6. ______ to visit us.
(Bitte veranlassen Sie, dass ein Vertreter uns besucht.)

4 **Your boss at Tiefhoch, Mr Clemens, wants you to write to Ro AS and gives you the notes below. Use the headed notepaper to write a letter.**

TIEFHOCH AG

Ruhrtalstr. 21
D-45127 Essen
Germany

Tel: +49 (0)201/4 37 38-0
E-Mail: info@tiefhoch.de
Web: www.tiefhoch.de

Ref: __________

Date: __________

Ro AS

Dear __________

- Bitte einen Brief an Ro AS schreiben
- Betreff: Produktanfrage
- Ihre Anzeige im European Construction Journal vom ... (Datum) hat uns interessiert
- Wir sind eine führende deutsche Baufirma mit Sitz in Essen, weltweit tätig
- Weitere Infos auf unserer Website
- Bitte aktuelle Verkaufsprospekte / Preisliste senden, sowie zum Testen Muster Ihrer Produkte
- Bitte auch Angaben zu Rabatten, Lieferzeiten und Zahlungsbedingungen
- Sollten Ihre Produkte konkurrenzfähig sein, werden wir möglicherweise große Mengen kaufen
- Wir würden uns freuen bald von Ihnen zu hören usw.

(Your name)

Assistant to Mr Nils Clemens, Purchasing Manager

5 **Mr Clemens is on a business trip in England. He sends you this email. Write the letter on a separate piece of paper.**

Von: n.clemens@tiefhoch.de
Gesendet: 18. Februar 20 _ _ 17:01
An: yourname@tiefhoch.de
Betreff: Bitte Produktanfrage schreiben

Liebe(r) *(Your name)*,

gestern auf der Messe in Birmingham habe ich die Produkte der britischen Firma Danbury Windows Ltd. angesehen. Das Unternehmen stellt hervorragende PVC-Fenster her und ich würde gern eine Anfrage an die Firma schicken, um weitere Infos zu erhalten. Außerdem könnte Danbury Windows veranlassen, dass ein Vertreter aus ihrem Verkaufsbüro in Deutschland uns in Essen besucht. Bitte direkt an die Zentrale in London schreiben (101 Lewes Avenue, London NW3 4WW, an die Verkaufsleiterin Frau Jane Appleyard). Bitten Sie um aktuelle Verkaufsprospekte und eine Preisliste, und erkundigen Sie sich dann wegen des Vertreterbesuchs.

Hoffentlich läuft alles gut im Büro. Bis Montag.

Nils

6 ROUNDUP **Use the mindmap to collect words and phrases about letters of enquiry and B2B (Business to Business) commerce. Write in as many words and phrases as you can. Compare your mindmap afterwards with a partner's.**

ENQUIRIES

Where you find out about firms and their products

trade fairs

Ways to describe your company

medium-sized

Information a company can send you

possible discounts

Other things you may ask the firm for

visit from a representative

7 Marketing and the media

A Young experts talking

→ SB: S. 60–61

1 **The text below describes a company and a new product. Complete it with words from the box.**
EXTRA **Translate the completed article afterwards into German.**

advertising campaign • brand image • competitors • feature • market research • ~~market share~~ • medium • new media • posters • press • product • stood out • target group • to advertise • to target

Claggan's 'Energy' cereal bar

Background
Claggan Ltd. is a medium-sized Scottish company based in Edinburgh. Founded in 1993, Claggan's first product was muesli. With high-quality ingredients, the muesli became popular not only in Scotland but across the UK. In 2007, Claggan also started producing cereal bars. Sales were not as good as the company hoped. In 2009, after two years, Claggan's **(1)** market share of the UK cereal bar market was still only 3 per cent. They needed a new **(2)** ______________ .

Claggan's original cereal bar

Finding something 'different'
What should this new product be? The problem for Claggan was that it had several **(3)** ______________ , some of them large, international companies. Claggan needed a product that was 'different' from theirs – that **(4)** ______________ . Of course, the company carried out **(5)** ______________ constantly, and from this it knew the sorts of people who bought cereal bars. Most were women or children. Claggan decided **(6)** ______________ young, active men instead.

The 'Energy' bar is born
What kind of product would this **(7)** ______________ of young men want? Claggan decided on a 'sportsbar', a cereal bar whose special **(8)** ______________ was that is was full of protein. The **(9)** ______________ of the new bar was: 'clean, masculine, sporty'.

Selling the Energy bar
Six months later, the new bar was ready for sale. Now the company had **(10)** ______________ it. In its **(11)** ______________ , Claggan used more than one advertising **(12)** ______________ . It used **(13)** ______________ in the street and put advertisements in the **(14)** ______________ – mostly in young men's fitness magazines. It also used the **(15)** ______________ , with advertisements on the internet. At the end of the first year, the company knew the new Energy bar was a big hit. Claggan's market share had gone from 3 per cent to 15 per cent – a wonderful success story.

The new 'Energy' bar

► **cereal bar** *Müsliriegel* ► **background** *Hintergrund* ► **ingredients** *Zutaten* ► **constantly** *ständig*

B Language toolbox: Describing products and services → SB: S. 62–63, GS: F

1 Try this MONSTER exercise! Complete the sentences with the correct form of the word – adjective or adverb. In the grid on the right, tick (✓) the boxes for which sort of word you have used. Finish the exercise before checking the answers. If you can get it 100% right, you're an EXPERT!

ADJ. ADV.

1. **large:** I work for a large company in Germany. ✓
2. **famous:** The company is ____________ for its electronic products.
3. **easy:** You can buy many things very ____________ online today.
4. **quick:** When you order things online they usually arrive ____________.
5. **interesting:** I read this ____________ book last week about marketing.
6. **amazing:** The author had some ____________ ideas.
7. **excellent:** This is an ____________ new product.
8. **interested:** I think people will be very ____________ in it.
9. **careful:** Be ____________ when you cross the street in England.
10. **careful:** Always cross the street ____________ in England.
11. **automatic:** This is an ____________ door.
12. **automatic:** It opens ____________ when you're near it.
13. **extreme:** The company's customer service department is ____________ good.
14. **amazing:** They're ____________ efficient.
15. **total:** Lots of people think George is ____________ crazy.
16. **incredible:** In fact, he's ____________ clever.
17. **lovely:** Thanks for the flowers you sent. They're ____________!
18. **wonderful:** They smell ____________!
19. **strange:** Is there something wrong with your car, Jane? It sounds ____________.
20. **fast:** Jane likes ____________ cars.
21. **fast:** Unfortunately, she drives too ____________ in them.
22. **terrible:** I'm afraid that one day she'll have a ____________ accident.
23. **terrible:** It can be ____________ difficult to speak to Alison. She's always busy.
24. **fantastic:** Wow! The packaging looks ____________!
25. **simple:** The text of an advertisement should be as ____________ as possible.
26. **simple/clear:** Always write ____________ and ____________.
27. **fantastic/fast:** It's ____________ successful. People are buying it ____________.
28. **easy/complicated:** People should be able to understand a report ____________.
    This is much too ____________.
29. **clever / simple / awful / immediate:** I get a lot of sales letters through my letter box. Some of them are quite ____________. Others are ____________ ____________.
    Those are the ones I throw ____________ into my rubbish bin.
30. **immediate / friendly / real / funny:** Everyone who meets Simon likes him ____________. He always looks ____________ and when you talk to him, he often says ____________ ____________ things.

D Business topics

→ SB: S. 66–69

1 **What's this? Jake works for an advertising agency in London. He's talking to a group of German college students who are visiting his office. He has a quiz for them about advertising. Write in the answers.**

1. It's a kind of advertisement you find on the internet. It 'pops up' suddenly when you're browsing online.
   a pop-up (ad)
2. It's a sort of advertisement you see on TV. A number of them usually come together between programmes.
   ______
3. It's a type of advertisement you find on the internet. It's the oldest kind of online ad. You find it at the top of a web page.
   ______
4. It's a kind of advertising you sometimes find in computer games. Advertisers 'place' products in the games.
   ______
5. It's a sort of advertisement you see in the street. It's a large piece of paper. ______

2 **Now YOU. Write two (or more) sentences about each of these things. Use information from the text in your book (pages 66–67). Don't simply copy from the text. Try to use your own words and ideas.**

1. **a unicast ad**
   It's a kind of
2. **product placement**
3. **blogvertising**
4. **an email newsletter**
5. **dayparting**

It's a kind of / sort of / type of …

A good way to describe or define something is with the phrases: *A(n) … is a kind of / sort of / type of …*

What's a 'sidebar ad'?
– It's a kind of advertisement you find on a website.

3 **Use the expressions in the box to answer the questions below. Use your own words and ideas.**

1. Why is web advertising growing so quickly?

(I think) it's growing so quickly because

2. Why is it important to target specific groups when you advertise a product?

3. Why do you think there is so much advertising in the modern world?

Giving reasons

Here are some ways to answer questions with *Why ... ?*

- **because**
  We see a lot of ads every day ***because*** *they are everywhere.*
- **because of + noun**
  Everyone knows this product ***because of*** *the great ads for it.*
  (= aufgrund, wegen)
- **The (main) reason / One reason / Another reason why ... is that ...**
  The main reason why *pop-ups are annoying* ***is that*** *they appear when you don't want them.*
  (= Der (Haupt)grund / Ein (weiterer) Grund, warum ...)

EXTRA Analysing advertisements

When you want to analyse an advertisement, you need to think of the following things.

- What is the product or service that is being advertised?
- What is the advertising medium (e.g. a poster, an internet pop-up)?
- Who is the ad targeting – what is the product's target group – men, women, older people, ... ?
- What image of the product does the ad try to give – healthy, hi-tech, 'exclusive', not expensive, ...
- How does it try to do this – what 'devices' *(Instrumente)* does it use? Think of pictures, text and layout. An ad can be very complicated (with lots of text) or very simple. It can use humour. It can have lots of 'white space' ...
- What do you think of the ad yourself – what reaction(s) do you have to it? Do you find it successful? Awful (for example, you may find it sexist or silly). Is it clever? Remember – it targets a specific group, and you may not be in that group!

4 **One of the most important parts of an advertisement will be the brand image of the product. List as many words and phrases as you can that describe products or services. Use your dictionary if necessary.**

healthy, hi-tech, exclusive, not expensive (cheap)

5 Use the mindmap below to analyse these advertisements.
(Make more copies of the mindmap if necessary).

ADVERTISEMENT

Product or service

Medium

Target group

Brand image

Device(s)

Your reactions

Video lounge

→ SB: S. 69, Schüler DVD V3, Schüler DVD-Transkript

1 **Before you watch the video, read this text.**

eBay is an online auction *(Auktion)* site that brings buyers and sellers together. It claims *(behauptet)* that it's a safe place to trade. It protects *(schützt)* its users with a feedback system *(Rückmeldungen)*. Users rate *(bewerten)* each other's trustworthiness *(Vertrauenswürdigkeit)*. In online transactions *(Geschäftsvorgänge)*, one way to pay is with a money transfer *(Überweisung)*. eBay says that if something goes wrong, and a seller is at fault *(schuldig sein)*, it will refund *(zurückzahlen)* the money that buyers have parted with *(ausgegeben haben)*. People who buy things on eBay hope, of course, that the sellers will be legitimate *(seriös)*, that the system is secure *(sicher, verlässlich)* and that if there's a problem, eBay will cover them *(versichern)*. They should never be out of pocket *(bei einem Geschäft Verluste machen)*. eBay should not be a place where there is fraud *(Betrug)*, and you shouldn't meet fraudsters *(Betrüger)* and scammers who send you fake *(gefälschte)* emails or use hoaxes *(Tricks)* to rob you *(berauben)*. So how would you feel if the system didn't work and you lost money? Well, you may feel disgusted *(empört)*, upset *(bestürzt)*, furious *(wütend)* or – to use a slang word – 'gutted' *(herb enttäuscht)*. The one thing you don't want is a load of *(ein Haufen)* 'trouble and strife' *(Ärger und Streit)*.

2 **Now watch and make notes. What did James, Dave and Drew want to buy? What happened? How did each one feel afterwards? Why?**

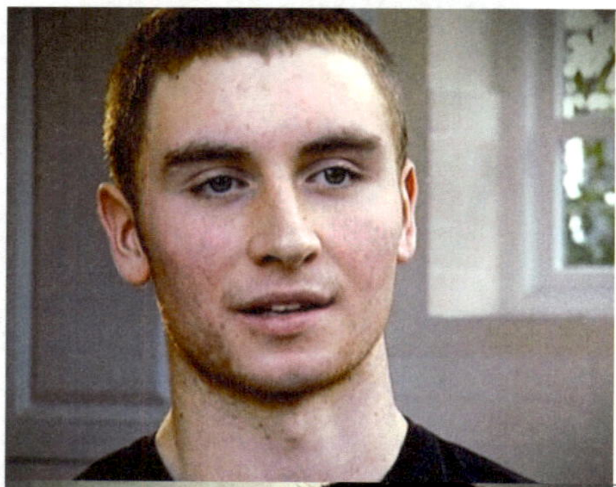

James McHardy

Dave Oram

Drew Dyer

3 EXTRA **Imagine you're James or Dave or Drew. Write a letter or email to eBay to protest about what has happened.**

8 Offers and orders

SITUATION
Founded only two years ago, Secret Forest GmbH is a medium-sized company based in Frankfurt. It produces luxury, handmade aromatherapy oils. The market for aromatherapy oils is growing rapidly around Europe, and in just two years, Secret Forest's range of products has become highly successful. You work in the sales department, where your boss, Michaela Frowein, is one of the founders of the company.

1 **This morning, you receive an enquiry by fax from a Spanish company. Make notes in German to summarise it for Frau Frowein.**

ESTETICA SL

C/ Calderon de la Barca, 1
03201 Alicante
Spain
Fax: +34-966 229 100

Fax message

To	From	Subject	Date	Pages
Secret Forest GmbH Nelkenstr. 81 60386 Frankfurt am Main, Germany	Ernesto Alvarez, Purchasing Dept.	Product enquiry	3 October 20 _ _	(incl. this page) 1

Dear Sirs

A number of our German and British customers have recently recommended your products to us.

Estetica is a chain of beauty salons which are located mainly in tourist hotels throughout Spain. In all, there are over 40 Estetica salons. Our head office is in Alicante.

Could you please send us your current sales brochure and price lists? Please let us know about possible discounts that you can offer, your terms of payment and your delivery times. We would also like to receive samples of your products to test. As we are a major player in the Spanish beauty industry, if your prices and quality are satisfactory, we may buy large quantities of your oils.

Yours faithfully

Ernesto Alvarez

Ernesto Alvarez
Purchasing Manager, Estetica SL

► **as** *da* ► **major player** *hier: bedeutendes Unternehmen*

2 Read the box about making an offer, then write as many expressions as you can into the mindmap.

MAKING AN OFFER

Before a company can reply to a letter of enquiry with its offer, it must decide a number of important things.

- **Transport:** How will it transport the goods? By sea? By air? …?
- **Price:** What is the basic price of the goods and what transport (or other costs) will it include in the final price that the buyer pays? Will the buyer perhaps pay a lower price than this, for example, if it places a large order?
- **Payment:** How (and when) should the buyer pay for the goods?
- **Delivery:** When will the company be able to deliver its goods to the buyer?

MAKING AN OFFER

Transport

company can transport the goods by sea / by air /

Price

basic price = EXW (ex-works) price
- price can include transport / freight

Payment

company can give the buyer credit / it can ask for cash in advance /

Delivery

company can send / deliver / dispatch the goods

3 EXTRA Incoterms **Read about how Secret Forest will deliver its products to Estetica (if Estetica decides to buy them), then write in the other incoterms.**

→ SB: S. 190 – 191

Whenever possible, Secret Forest tries to deliver its products by rail. If Estetica places an order, Secret Forest will load a container on to a train in Frankfurt. The consignment will then go directly to Valencia, about 130 kilometres from Alicante. Secret Forest will pay all the transport and insurance costs to this named place. The incoterm for this is:

CIP (Valencia): Carriage and Insurance Paid to Valencia

1. If the seller sends goods by road, rail or air and delivers to a named place in the buyer's country (e.g. Valencia) but *doesn't* pay for insurance, the incoterm is: ______

2. The seller arranges to send goods by sea (maritime transport) but pays only to deliver the goods to a port (e.g. Hamburg) in its own country. It doesn't pay for loading on to the ship.
   The correct incoterm is: ______

3. If the same seller as in 2 now also pays for loading the goods on to the ship in Hamburg, the incoterm is: ______

4. This incoterm is for all modes of transport and it's the best one for the buyer. It's when the seller delivers goods right to the seller – pays all costs, in other words – and also pays the duty (taxes) on the goods.
   It's ______

5. A company that is selling goods sends them by sea to a port in the buyer's country (e.g. Boston). If the seller pays the costs of unloading the goods in Boston, the incoterm will be ______. If not, it will be ______.

6. Commodities – mass volume products like wheat *(Weizen)* or coffee beans – need their own incoterm when they go by sea, and the seller pays for their transportation to a port but not for their unloading.
   It's ______.

4 EXTRA **Making business decisions. Make *if*-sentences Type 1 with the phrases below. Write on a separate piece of paper.** → GS: B2

If a company gives a potential customer a large discount, …
But if the discount is too large, …

the customer / be / more likely / to buy the product
the customer / also / perhaps / buy / more products in the future
the customer / perhaps / recommend / the products to others
the firm / not / make a profit
the customer / perhaps / think the products / aren't very good (high prices often mean high quality)

***If*-sentences Type 1**

People in business need to make decisions constantly – for example, about how much discount to give. A good way to talk about decisions is with an *if*-sentence Type 1:

if + simple present	***will*** future
If we **give** them a big discount,	they**'ll** (perhaps) **buy** our products.

5 **Your boss Frau Frowein wants you to reply to Estetica's enquiry and she gives you their fax with some notes. Below the fax are some phrases you can use when you write your letter. First, put them in the correct order (write 1, 2, 3, . . .), then add the necessary information.**

Dear Sirs

A number of our German and British customers have recently recommended your products to us. *Vielen Dank für Ihre Anfrage vom. 3. Okt.*

Estetica is a chain of beauty salons which are located mainly in tourist hotels throughout Spain. In all, there are over 40 Estetica salons. Our head office is Alicante.

Anbei. Alle Preise CIP (Valencia)

Could you please send us your current sales brochure and price lists? Please let us know about possible discounts that you can offer, your terms of payment and your delivery times.

10 % Einführungsrabatt

bei Auftragserteilung

innerhalb von 21 Tagen nach Erhalt der Bestellung

We would also like to receive samples of your products to test. As we are a major player in the Spanish beauty industry, if your prices and quality are satisfactory, we may buy large quantities of your oils.

schicken wir sofort

Yours faithfully
Ernesto Alvarez

Ernesto Alvarez
Purchasing Manager, Estetica SL

- Angebot 3 Monate gültig
- Sie können sicher sein ...
- Wir freuen uns ...

_____ We are pleased to offer you _____

_1_ Thank you very much for _your enquiry of 3 October._

_____ For a first order _____

_____ Enclosed are _____

_____ All prices are _____

_____ This quotation is valid _____

_____ We assure you that _____

_____ The goods will be dispatched _____

_____ As you requested, we are sending you immediately _____

_____ We look forward _____

6 **Below and on the next page are more phrases that you can use in an offer. What are the missing English words?**

1. We are pleased to quote _as follows_.
   (Wir freuen uns, Ihnen folgendes Angebot machen zu können.)
2. We are _____ (or: _____) to offer you . . .
   (Wir sind bereit, Ihnen . . . zu gewähren.)

3. … a ______________________________ of 5% off list price.
(… einen Mengenrabatt von 5% gegenüber dem Listenpreis.)

4. Delivery will be made ______________________________ .
(Die Lieferung erfolgt sofort nach Erhalt der Bestellung.)

5. Thank you again for your ______________________________ .
(Wir danken Ihnen nochmals für Ihr Interesse an unseren Produkten.)

6. If you have any further questions, please ______________________________ .
(Sollten Sie weitere Fragen haben, zögern Sie bitte nicht, sich mit uns in Verbindung zu setzen.)

7 **Now write the letter to Estetica. Write on a separate piece of paper. Use the correct letter layout.** → SB: S. 56

8 **Two weeks later at Estetica, Mr Alvarez's secretary Carla Iglesias is placing an order for a consignment of Secret Forest products. She's writing the cover letter that she'll send with a purchase order. Below are some phrases that you often use in a letter like this – but at the moment the words are mixed up. Write the phrases correctly.**

1. **Thank you …**
you / for / your letter / you / thank / and the samples / of 4 October / sent us
Thank you for your letter of 4 October and the samples you sent us.

2. **Our purchase order**
enclosed / our purchase / 1234 / order / find / number / Please
____

3. **Confirming prices**
your offer / all / understand / are / that / We / from / DDP Aachen / your prices
____

4. **Confirming discount**
are / us / to offer / You / of / a discount / willing / 4%
____

5. **Confirming terms of payment**
30 days / order / should / of / made / be / Payment / receipt / within / after
____

6. **Confirming delivery**
order / We / delivery / 7 days / can / of / the / consignment / within / of / of / expect / receipt
____

7. **Confirming validity**
6 / offer / Your / for / valid / is / months
____

8. **Finishing your letter**
the / with / in / look / and / to / you / doing / receiving / We / forward / business / goods / time / further
____

9 Here is Carla's purchase order. First, write in the missing words on the order, then write the cover letter for it. Use the details from Secret Forest's offer.

ESTETICA SL

(1) PURCHASE ORDER No. 70/A/12

(2) ______________ 18 October 20 _ _

(3)	(4)	(5)	(6)	(7)
A17	Bergamot	5 litres	450	2,250
A20	Eucalyptus	5 litres	250	1,250
A45	Jasmine	1 litre	1,480	1,480
A63	Camomile (wild)	2 litres	1,380	2,760
A100	Lavender	10 litres	250	2,500
A112	Myrrh	3 litres	850	2,550
A130	Peppermint	1 litre	340	340
A146	Sandalwood	2 litres	3,390	6,780
A151	Thyme	2 litres	700	1,400
A175	Verbena	2 litres	790	1,580
(8)				22,890
(9)				2,289
(10)				€ **20,601**

10 ROUNDUP **Enquiry, offer or order? Write the key phrases from each type of letter in English into the table.**

- Danke für Ihren Katalog und die Muster, die Sie uns geschickt haben.
- Danke für Ihre Anfrage vom 9. Januar.
- Die Lieferung können wir innerhalb von einer Woche erwarten.
- Wir bitten um Zusendung Ihres aktuellen Verkaufsprospekts.
- Wir freuen uns darauf, Ihnen in Zukunft weitere Aufträge zu erteilen.
- Wir freuen uns, Ihnen einen Handelsrabatt von 5% anbieten zu können.
- Wir freuen uns, Ihnen folgendes Angebot unterbreiten zu können.
- Wir hoffen, dass dieses Angebot Ihren Erwartungen entspricht.
- ~~Sollten Ihre Preise konkurrenzfähig sein, werden wir möglicherweise große Mengen Ihrer Produkte kaufen.~~
- Wir möchten bestätigen, dass Sie einverstanden sind, uns einen Handelsrabatt von 5% zu gewähren.
- Wir würden auch gern mehr über Ihre Zahlungsbedingungen erfahren.
- Zahlung sollte innherhalb von 30 Tagen erfolgen.

Enquiries	Offers	Orders
If your prices are competitive, we may buy large quantities of your products		

9 Ecology and technology

A Young experts talking

→ SB: S. 80–81

1 Try this crossword about the environment.

DOWN

2 Coal, oil and gas are … *(two words)*
3 *Kraftwerk (two words)*
4 It surrounds our planet. (Tip: The first letter is A.)
5 *Klima*. The earth's … is changing.
6 When the earth is very, very dry.
7 The earth's average … is 15 °C at the moment.
10 Materials like wood and vegetables oils are …
11 CO_2 is … *(wird ausgestoßen)* when you burn coal or oil.
12 A place that Nadine's company plans and builds.
15 Floods and hurricanes are two forms of … weather.
17 … power = *Atomkraft*
18 The problem that everyone is talking about is global … *(die Erderwärmung)*

ACROSS

1 The opposite of 'dangerous'.
8 CO_2 … from the places in **3 DOWN** every year are around 1.5 billion tonnes.
9 Energy that you can use again and again is … *(nachhaltig)* energy.
13 CO_2 = carbon …
14 Energy from water is … energy.
16 The Arctic and Antarctic are the North and South …
19 *Treibhaus*. The … effect.
20 Energy you can renew is … energy.
21 Energy from the sun is … energy.
22 Scientists think that … energy will be the most important form of green energy in the next 20 years.
23 When people have nothing to eat.

B Language toolbox: Describing processes

→ SB: S. 82–83; GS: C

1 Find and underline all the passive forms, then write them into the table below.

The power of the wind has been used for at least 5,000 years. Before steamships, for example, most journeys by sea were made in sailing ships. Today, however, windpower is being used in a new way: to produce electricity. The first modern wind turbines *(Windkraftturbinen)* were built around 1980. Since then thousands more have been constructed around the world. Often, several wind turbines are placed together in a windpark or 'windfarm'. Many of these windparks are now being built at sea ('off-shore'), where the wind is strongest. Right now, only a relatively small percentage of the world's electricity is produced by windfarms, but wind energy is one of the fastest-growing green technologies, and experts believe that in the future, much more electricity will be produced in this way. In most European countries, targets have been set *(Ziele setzen)* for much higher levels *(Niveaus)* of wind energy. Some say that in 2030, between 30 and 40% of all our energy will be supplied by windpower. That means that more windfarms will be built, especially in Europe, in countries like Denmark and Germany, which are the world-leaders in wind energy technology.

simple present	simple past	*will* future	present perfect	present continuous
			has been used	

2 Complete this text with the correct passive forms of the verbs.

Solar panels on the roof of a house, southern Germany

A photovoltaic (PV) cell

Another form of alternative energy is solar power. Solar energy is energy that **(1)** is produced **(produce)** by sunlight. A photovoltaic (PV) cell can turn light into electricity. The idea of 'photovoltaics' **(2)** ______ **(discover)** by a French scientist in 1839, but the first modern solar panels **(3)** ______ **(manufacture)** only a long time later, in the 1950s. A country where solar technology is booming is Germany. One reason why Germans are using so much solar power today is that the industry **(4)** ______ **(support)** very actively by the government. Since the 1990s, 1.5 million solar power systems **(5)** ______ **(install)** in German houses, schools, offices, swimming pools and many other places. German manufacturers also export solar panels. German PV cells **(6)** ______ **(export)** around the world, many to much sunnier countries than Germany, like Africa. And the future? Solar power is a rapidly-growing industry and it is certain that more and more electricity **(7)** ______ **(produce)** this way in years to come.

► **discover** *entdecken* ► **boom** *anziehen, boomen* ► **support** *unterstützen* ► **install** *montieren*

3 **Look at the box then write the passive sentences. Underline the keyword in each sentence and think about 'singular' and 'plural' verbs.**

1. Around 60% of electricity is produced **(produce)** by coal fired power stations.
2. In the EU, around 12% of CO_2 ______ **(emit)** in our homes.
3. Before steamships, 99% of sea journeys ______ **(make)** in sailing ships.
4. 30% of all the oranges in the world ______ **(grow)** in Brazil.
5. 100% of the products in your local supermarket ______ **(transport)** there by lorry.
6. Last year, 80% of the flowers on sale in British supermarkets ______ **(produce)** in Kenya.
7. Only a small percentage of freight in the EU ______ **(transport)** by air.
8. Experts believe that in 2050, 100% more goods ______ **(transport)** around the world than today.
9. Germany is a large wine producer. Around 70% of the wine that ______ **(produce)** in Germany is white wine.

Talking about percentages

You use singular ***and*** plural verbs with percentages! It depends on the thing(s) you are talking about:

- *24% of our **energy*** (singular) ***is*** *produced by windfarms etc.*
- *44% of **goods*** (plural) ***are*** *transported by road.*

4 **Complete this text about containers with passive forms of the verbs. Be careful! Most forms are a passive infinitive.**

Goods **(1)** have been transported **(transport)** by sea for thousands of years, but in 1955, something happened that revolutionised freight transport: the container **(2)** ______ **(invent)**. It was the idea of Malcolm McLean, an American who had a small trucking company *(Fuhrunternehmen)*. McLean started using a standard sized box for all his consignments. These boxes (they **(3)** ______ **(name)** 'containers') could **(4)** ______ **(load)** directly from his trucks on to (and off) ships. Why was this such an innovative *(bahnbrechend)* idea? The first reason is that a container can **(5)** ______ **(transport)** by road, rail or sea and the goods can stay in the container. Before they **(6)** ______ **(invent)**, hundreds of different items had **(7)** ______ **(load)** – and then unloaded – separately. The second reason is that containers have dramatically reduced transport costs. Before McLean's invention, it took days to load and unload a ship in port. Today, in a major port such as Hamburg, a container ship can **(8)** ______ **(unload)** in 4–5 hours. The items don't need **(9)** ______ **(handle** *abfertigen*) individually.

The third reason is that goods in containers are safe. They can't **(10)** ______ **(damage)** by sea water, they can't **(11)** ______ **(steal)** easily, and they are much less likely **(12)** ______ **(break)**. Containers don't seem at first to be an exciting business idea. But commerce as we know it today couldn't function without them.

D Business topics

1 **Practise writing about the advantages and disadvantages (the 'pros and cons') of different kinds of alternative fuels for cars. First, match the advantages and disadvantages of each fuel in the table, then continue the text below in your own words. Use the expressions in your book on page 82 and the extra expressions in the box below.**

Type of fuel	Advantages	Disadvantages
Electricity	**1** Fuels are 'carbon neutral'.	**a** Both fuels still produce some CO_2 (not a perfect solution).
CNG / LPG	**2** Cars produce no CO_2 at all.	**b** People in poorer countries grow plants for these fuels when they should grow food.
Ethanol / biofuel	**3** Cars produce a lot less CO_2 than 'normal' cars; 'normal' cars can be easily converted to use these fuels.	**c** Fuel comes from power stations (which pollute); cars are slow.

Electricity	2c	CNG / LPG		Ethanol / biofuel	

Pros and cons	
Advantages The (big) advantage of … is that … … has the advantage that … The good thing about … is that … The good news about … is that … On the plus side, … is/are … While/whereas *(indem)* … is/are …, Although … is/are …,	**Disadvantages** The (big) disadvantage (of …) is that … It has the disadvantage, however, that … The bad thing / problem is that … The bad news is that … The downside is that it is / they are … It is / they are also … It is / they are unfortunately also …

It is very clear that cars that use gas (petrol) are a major source of CO_2 emissions and therefore play an important role in global warming. So what alternative fuels are available, and what are the pros and cons of each? The first alternative fuel is electricity. There have been electric cars for some years now so they are not a new idea. The big advantage of

2 EXTRA **Nanotechnology is a new technology that will change our lives. But how much do you know about modern technology generally? When were things invented? Where? By whom? Try this quiz!**

1. It is probably one of the most famous events in modern history – Wilbur and his brother Orville's first flight in an aeroplane. But when was it?

   ☐ **a** 1899 ☐ **b** 1903 ☐ **c** 1910?

2. Henry Ford revolutionised transport with the first mass-produced automobile, the Model-T Ford. But when was the first Model-T manufactured?

   ☐ **a** 1908 ☐ **b** 1920 ☐ **c** 1931

3. In 1925, a Scotsman called John Logie Baird introduced the world to an amazing new technology. What was it?

   ☐ **a** telephones ☐ **b** telepathy ☐ **c** television

4. The history of computers is very complicated and we can't say that one person invented them alone. Here are some important milestones, however. Can you match the dates and the events?

   1958 • 1964 • 1981 • 1985

   ______ the invention of the 'mouse'

   ______ first Microsoft Windows

   ______ first silicon chip

   ______ first home computer

   BONUS POINT Who is the inventor of the Microsoft Windows program?

   ____

5. Our modern world would be very different without a man called Dr Martin Cooper. He invented the modern mobile phone. But when was the first call made by Dr Cooper?

   ☐ **a** 1953 ☐ **b** 1973 ☐ **c** 1993?

   BONUS POINT In which city was the call made?

   ____

6. It is really impossible to imagine modern business without emails. But when was the first 'electronic message' sent between two computers?

   ☐ **a** 1951 ☐ **b** 1961 ☐ **c** 1971

7. YouTube was founded in the U.S. by Chad Hurley, Steve Chen and Jawed Karim. When?

   ☐ **a** 2002 ☐ **b** 2004 ☐ **c** 2006

8. When it was invented, an 'expert' said that women could never use it. What was it?

   ☐ **a** the washing machine
   ☐ **b** the typewriter
   ☐ **c** the telephone

► **milestone** *Meilenstein*

3 EXTRA **Look at the text about containers in your workbook on page 49. Use it as a model to write a short text about *one* of the inventions in the quiz above. How has it changed the world (of business)?**

____

____

____

____

____

____

____

____

____

____

Video lounge

→ SB: S. 89, DVD V4, Schüler DVD-Transkript

People you'll meet and places you'll hear about in the video

John Craven

Richard Sadler

Sir Bernard Ingham

Lancashire, Yorkshire and Northumberland are three English counties. Blyth is a town in Northumberland. East Anglia is a region in eastern England.

This video is from a BBC series called *Countryfile*. It reports on the countryside and the environment. John Craven and Richard Sadler are its regular presenters. A guest on the programme this week is Sir Bernard Ingham. In the 1980s and 90s, he was the press secretary *(Pressesprecher)* of the famous British prime minister Mrs Thatcher. The programme was broadcast in 2000, at a time when windfarms were still a new idea in the UK.

Part 1 of the programme: Windfarms in the UK and Denmark

1. John Craven starts the programme. Can you fill in the missing words?

"Are we about to witness a **(1)** ____________________ in Britain's energy policy? *Countryfile* has learned the government is drawing up plans for a major **(2)** ____________________ of wind power to meet its commitment to cut back on **(3)** ____________________. Licences are expected to be granted this summer for about a **(4)** ____________________ wind farms around our coastline. And for the first time planners have been told to draw up targets for **(5)** ____________________ as well."

► **witness** *miterleben* ► **commitment** *Verpflichtung* ► **cut back on** *einschränken*

2. Richard Sadler explains that the power of the wind has been harnessed *(sich etw. zunutze machen)* for thousands of years. What does he say next about these things?
   - **a** the potential of windpower in the 21st century
   - **b** Britain's first offshore windfarm at Blyth in Northumberland
   - **c** plans for more wind farms
   - **d** Britain on the verge of *(kurz davor sein)* a new North Sea bonanza *(Glücksfall)*
3. Sadler talks next about Denmark.
   - **a** What target has the Danish government set for wind energy by 2030?
   - **b** Britain is 'years behind the Danes'. But what advantage does Britain have?
   - **c** What does the company behind the Blyth project say about the next decade *(Jahrzehnt)*?

Part 2: The interview with Sir Bernard Ingham

1. Here are some useful words. Listen to Sir Bernard and note down his arguments against wind farms and wind energy.
2. Sadler finishes the programme like this. Complete the sentence. "Whatever the arguments for and against, investors are convinced Britain is now poised *(bereit)* for a major expansion in wind energy developments and it's just been confirmed that …"

to be conned *betrogen werden*
objection *Bedenken*
aesthetic *ästhetisch*
bang in the middle of *mitten drin*
wreck *vernichten*
gale *Sturm*

10 Complaints

Tomas Porvaznik is a management assistant with HB-Illumina GmbH, a company based in Dortmund that makes eco-friendly headlight *(Scheinwerfer)* bulbs for the German car industry. His boss is the production manager, Martin Werner. HB-Illumina has a regular supplier for its packaging, a British company called TotalBox Ltd., from which it orders monthly consignments of cardboard boxes *(Pappkartons)* of various sizes. This morning, however, Tomas has a memo from his boss. Something has gone wrong …

1 **Look at Herr Werner's notes and complete Tomas's email below with the missing information and phrases from the box.**

Tomas - Bitte TotalBox sofort per E-Mail eine Beschwerde schreiben - Lieferung für März (J-770-M) angekommen - sie haben uns 1.500 30 x 10 x 20 cm Kartons statt 1.500 30 x 10 x 10 cm geliefert - wichtiger Kunde von uns wartet nächsten Montag auf eine Lieferung - wir brauchen dringend die richtige Ware!

- instead of
- look into this matter for us
- replacements
- that we ordered
- This is a particular problem for us
- we need the packing boxes
- what you would like us to do with the incorrect boxes
- when we opened the container
- with reference to

An: davina.grant@totalbox_sales.co.uk
Kopie an: m.werner@hb-illumina.de
Betreff: URGENT! Problem with March consignment

Dear Ms Grant

I'm writing to you **(1)** *with reference to* our March consignment, our order number **(2)** __________.

The consignment arrived yesterday. However, **(3)** __________, we found that it contained 1,500 30x10x*20* cm boxes **(4)** __________ the 1,500 30x10x **(5)** __________ cartons **(6)** __________. The other items were correct.

(7) __________ because an important customer is expecting a delivery from us **(8)** __________ and **(9)** __________ so that we can dispatch their goods.

Could you please **(10)** __________ immediately and send us **(11)** __________ as soon as possible – at the latest by this Thursday? As we do not normally use boxes of the size that you have sent us by mistake, could you also please let us know **(12)** __________.

Best regards
Tomas Porvaznik
Assistant to Martin Werner, Production Manager

2 Use the flowchart diagrams below and on the next page to practise writing complaints and replies to complaints. Write as many letters or emails as you want until you feel confident *(sicher)*. Invent details yourself. Add key phrases to the diagrams to help you to remember them.

COMPLAINTS

I'm writing … / I'm afraid I have to write to you …

The goods arrived but …

when we opened the crates we found that

broken

wrong

missing

some items were

don't work

customers have complained

The goods haven't arrived …

due on …

Problem for us because …

Please look into this matter urgently and …

- replacements
- the old goods?

Problem for us because …

Immediate dispatch please!

Regards …

REPLIES TO COMPLAINTS

Sorry …

the goods were broken, wrong, don't work

You haven't received your goods

We've looked into the matter …

The reason is …

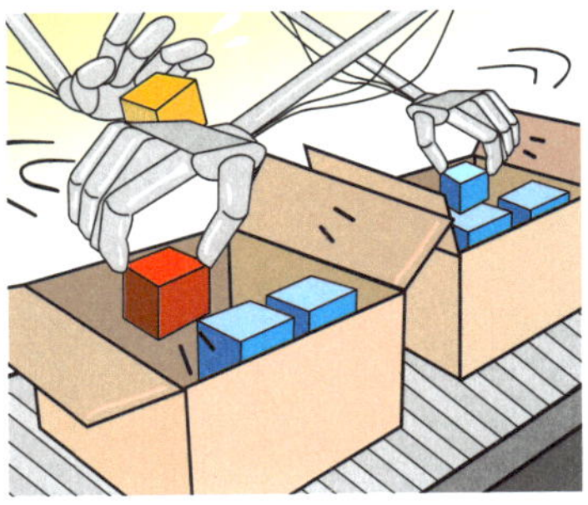

Mixup

Busy!

Problem with supplier!

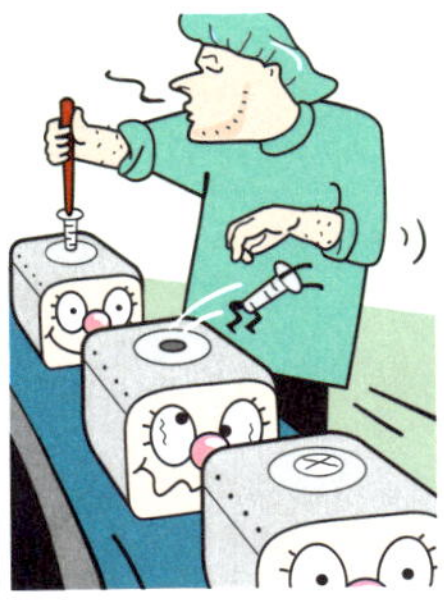

Problem with production

- We're sending …
- Please keep / return …

We're sending …

Sorry again!

Regards …

3 EXTRA Here are some more words and expressions for complaints. Use your dictionary if necessary to write in their German meanings.

How goods can be damaged		
They can be:	torn	zerrissen
	warped	
	scratched	
	bent	
	water-damaged	
	cracked	
	corroded	
	damaged in transit	
	damaged because the packaging has broken open	
Other problems		
The goods	don't meet our specifications	
	can't be sold	
	are useless to us	
Late delivery		
Our order is	now 10 days overdue	
Please send our goods	without delay	

4 ROUNDUP Can you give the German meanings of all these key words and phrases without needing to check?

1. admit (you are wrong)	zugeben
2. apologise (for)	
3. assure (s.o. that)	
4. at our expense	
5. be forced to	
6. cancel (an order)	
7. crate	
8. (delivery was) due	
9. due to	
10. express (our) regret	
11. faulty	
12. (show) good will	

13. immediate dispatch	
14. inconvenient	
15. inspect (goods)	
16. instead of	
17. look into (a problem)	
18. make a complaint	
19. mix up *(noun)*	
20. put sthg. right	
21. replacement(s)	
22. slightly (damaged)	
23. temporary (difficulties)	
24. (not) up to standard	

5 Write four or five sentences with the expressions in (exercise) 4 to show how they are used. You can put more than one expression into each sentence.

1. When you receive a complaint from a customer, you should admit you are wrong, apologise for the mistake, then put things right.

11 Industry, service and trade (1)

A Young experts talking

→ SB: S. 98–99

1 **First match the words and the definitions, then choose at least *six* words and write a sentence with each. Use your own ideas – don't copy sentences from your book. Continue on a separate piece of paper if necessary.**

1 boom (v.)
2 revolutionise (v.)
3 unemployment (n.)
4 survive (v.)
5 regeneration (n.)
6 sector (n.)
7 dominant (adj.)
8 income (n.)
9 shift (n.)
10 industrialisation (n.)
11 post-industrialisation (n.)
12 decline (v.)
13 increase (v.)
14 demand (n.)
15 needs (n. pl.)

a *(economics)* when people want to buy products there is a ~ for the products
b a movement from one place or situation to another
c be very successful, grow quickly
d become larger and more important
e become smaller and less important
f becoming alive again (after being dead, dirty, old etc.)
g completely change sthg. (so it becomes better)
h continue to live, not die
i most important, strongest
j part of sthg., e.g. the industrial ~
k the money people earn is their ~
l the process whereby industries become less important and services more important in a country's economy
m the process whereby agriculture becomes less important and industries more important in a country's economy
n the things people must have are their ~
o a situation when people have no jobs

1 c 2 3 4 5 6 7 8

9 10 11 12 13 14 15

Topics you could write about: the internet / cinema / TV / music • a town or city you know well • richer (developed) and poorer (developing) countries • people in your family or people you know (especially older people) • new products and gadgets • clothes and fashions • different types of companies • the (world / German) economy at the moment • another country you know well • the things that are important to you in your everyday life • some products that are now out-of-date • your ideas about life in the future • an area of business you know about

1. Internet shopping - buying goods online - is booming at the moment.
2.

B Language toolbox: Describing change

→ SB: S.100–101; GS: A

1 **Benedikt Knüttel is the manager of one of Germany's airports. He's talking about the changes to the airport past, present and future. Give the right headings for the four speech bubbles. Write in A, B, C or D.**

B Was sich in letzter Zeit geändert hat

____ Aktuelle Änderungen, die im Moment ablaufen

____ Wie es in der Zukunft weitergeht

____ Wie es früher war

A The airport was built in the 1950s and until five years ago it was quite small.

B It has grown dramatically in the last five years because of a modernisation and expansion programme.

C We're currently building a new hotel and conference centre near the airport, so things are still changing.

D My hope is that in a couple of years from now, we'll be one of Germany's busiest regional airports.

2 **Julie Carr manages a shopping centre in the UK. Complete what she says with the correct forms of the verbs.**

The retail industry (1) has changed **(change)** dramatically in the last few years. Here in my hometown 20 years ago, most shops (2) ______ **(be)** relatively small and most (3) ______ **(be)** family owned. But since the 1990s, the importance of these smaller shops (4) ______ **(decline)** and many (5) ______ **(disappear)**. The shopping centre which I manage (6) ______ **(be/built** ***TIP: active or passive?*****)** in 2002. Business is booming and right now we (7) ______ **(expand)** the centre with ten new stores. We (8) ______ also ______ **(improve)** the café and restaurant facilities with a new coffee shop and a sushi bar. The town council has some interesting plans for the future, too. If all goes well, in the next five years or so they (9) ______ **(build)** a new leisure centre right next to us and possibly there (10) ______ **(be)** a new cinema. My hope is that these (11) ______ **(attract)** even more shoppers.

► **town council** *Stadtverwaltung*

3 Fewer or less? Complete the sentences.

→ SB: S.100–101; GS: G

Changing lifestyles

1. Smoking is now banned in most public places and fewer people smoke than in the past.
2. Careers can be hectic in the modern world and on average people spend ______ time with their families than 20 years ago.
3. People take more holidays nowadays than in the past but ______ holidays are booked through travel agents. There has been a shift to online booking.
4. Today, many shops are open seven days a week. In the past, far ______ shops opened in the evenings or at the weekend.
5. Eating out is booming. 20 years ago, people spent a lot ______ money in restaurants than they do now.
6. When video technology first appeared, people said the cinema couldn't survive – people would watch ______ films. In fact, going to a movie is still an immensely popular leisure activity.

4 **Jason Kitango is an ex-professional *(ehemaliger ...)* footballer who lives in London. He now runs an e-commerce company that sells its own brand of sports clothing. He's talking about his company. Underline the correct words in the sentences.**

1. When I started the company I had *little / few* experience of business.
2. I discussed my ideas at the beginning with *a few / a little* friends.
3. We sold only *a few / a little* clothes in the first month.
4. I had very *little / few* money to spend on advertising and most of our advertising was word of mouth.
5. Sales increased dramatically after six months and we were constantly busy. I had very *little / few* free time.
6. Business is booming now. Last month, we sold *the most / the fewest* clothes we have ever sold in one month.
7. Since we began, we have had *the most / the least / the fewest* success with our sales to professional clubs. They all buy a lot of clothing from us. We have had *the most / the least / the fewest* success with children's clothing. Parents can buy these relatively cheaply from big stores.

5 **Write sentences with *the number / amount of* and the verbs *rise, grow, expand, increase, fall, drop, shrink, decrease* and *decline*.**

1. The number of people in agriculture ↘ has declined in recent years.
2. The ______ of women who work ↗ ______ since the 1950s.
3. The ______ of money we spend on leisure ↗ ______ in the last few years, too.
4. The ______ of pollution from factories ↘ ______ enormously since 1900.
5. The ______ small firms in the EU ↗ ______ recently.
6. The ______ of software available ↗ ______ rapidly in recent years.
7. The ______ interest in our products ↘ ______ dramatically, I'm afraid.

The number / amount of ...

You use *the number of* (die Anzahl von) to talk about countable things and *the amount of* (die Menge, Quantität von) to talk about uncountable things:

*The **number** of people who came to the meeting*
*The **amount** of time we spend*

D Business topics

→ SB: S. 104–107

1 Explaining. Read the tips in the box then practise explaining the terms below. You can write the sentences in several different ways. Use your own ideas and your dictionary if necessary.

1. **hotdesking**
   'Hotdesking' basically means sharing desks. It's when there are fewer desks in an office than people. Another more modern name for it is 'hotelling'.
2. **collaborating**
3. **co-worker**
3. **blue chip company**
4. **mobile wi-fi technology**
5. **wasted space**
6. **workplace**
7. **'formal' and 'informal' meetings**

Explaining

When you are speaking (or writing) you want your ideas to be clear. Sometimes, it is helpful to explain exactly what you mean. You can use the expressions below to do this:

X (basically) means …
X means that …
X is (basically) …
X is when …
Another word/term/expression/ name for X is …
In other words, …
An example of X is …
The idea behind X is …
The opposite of X is Y.

2 Your company is reviewing *(überprüfen)* its policy on corporate culture and you would like to refer to this magazine article at the next meeting. Read the article – use your dictionary if necessary – then copy and complete the grid below in German. You can write notes.

Company values

Schuster's Snacks Inc. began 15 years ago and for the last ten years it has consistently been in the list of Top 100 Places To Work in the USA. This is no huge blue chip company, however, but a medium-sized concern that employs 750 people and is based in the small midwestern town of Winesburg, Ohio. So what is its secret?

Bob Schuster, Schuster's Snacks Inc.'s founder and CEO. "It's important to let people in the company know what's going on."

If you worked at Schuster's Snacks ten years ago, the chances are that the faces of the people you met were all familiar. "When we first started up," explains Schuster's founder and CEO Bob Schuster, "most of our people were hired because they knew someone who worked here or were related to them. Everyone knew everyone."

At that time, the company workforce was 250 employees. Since then it has grown to 750 and its turnover from $4 million to over $700 million. But despite Schuster's rapid growth, it has been very careful to keep its original corporate culture. "Our core values are caring about people, caring about the product, and working hard," says Bob Schuster. "Good old Midwestern values."

The company takes specific steps to make sure that it hires the right people. Job applicants don't just get an interview. Schuster's HR team spends time with them to get to know them well and to find out if (and where) they would fit into the company. And once hired, new employees spend time again with the company's Culture Club, a group of people who have all been with the company since the beginning. These 'meetings' are actually more likely to be a pizza party or a round of golf, but the aim is to pass on to new recruits Schuster's attitudes and what it expects from its employees.

The other aspect of Schuster's culture that Bob and everyone else is clear about is the need for open communication. "There's no 'us and them' attitude here," says Mary Keller, one of the 75 people who started here 15 years ago. "Bob comes on to the shop floor all the time and it's quite normal for him to pick up a box and to start packing snacks. You see, that's how things are done here. Everybody helps everybody out when they need it."

"The key to a successful company is to talk to people and to be honest with them," explains Bob Schuster. "They are part of the company and it's important to let them know what's going on. And that includes financially. Everybody's bonus is based on our profits, and people need to know what they're likely to be."

Unternehmen (Sitz/Produkte/ Belegschaft/Geschichte/Umsatz)	
Grundwerte des Unternehmens	
Wie realisiert das Unternehmen seine Ziele?	
Wie hat die Firmenpolitik des Unternehmens zu seinem geschäftlichen Erfolg beigetragen?	

3 EXTRA **You find this article about changes in the workplace in Germany. As you will be meeting some English-speaking visitors to your office next week, and you know that they would be interested in the information in the article, you decide to summarise it in English. Write a summary in about 200 words in full sentences on a separate piece of paper.**

Das klassische Büro verändert sich

Millionen von deutschen Arbeitnehmern werden nach einer neuen Studie in naher Zukunft nicht mehr in einem klassischen Büro arbeiten. Schon heute sind rund sechs Millionen Beschäftigte ganz oder teilweise als Telearbeiter tätig, arbeiten also von zu Hause oder unterwegs. „Die Zahl der Menschen ohne festen Schreibtisch in einem eigenen Büro wird in den nächsten Jahren sehr stark zunehmen", sagt Katrin Strese, HR Beraterin. Einige Formen der Telearbeit hatten schon in den vergangenen Jahren Wachstumsraten von mehr als 50 Prozent. Die Gründe: veränderte Anforderungen der modernen Arbeitswelt und Kostendruck der Unternehmen. „Da man per Internet und E-Mail heute von jedem Platz der Welt aus arbeiten kann, ist die Anwesenheit von Montag bis Freitag im Büro oft nicht mehr nötig", sagt Strese. Entsprechend verkleinern Unternehmen ihre Büroflächen und senken so die Betriebskosten. Außerdem kommen die modernen Arbeitsformen jenen Beschäftigten entgegen, die Beruf und Familie vereinbaren wollen oder die wegen der niedrigeren Immobilienpreise lieber außerhalb der Ballungsräume wohnen.

Und so könnte die Arbeitswelt schon bald für Millionen von Bundesbürgern aussehen:

- Telearbeit: Man arbeitet von zu Hause aus oder beim Kunden (etwa als Unternehmensberater oder IT-Fachmann) und ist per Computer ständig mit seinem eigenen Unternehmen verbunden. Fast 17 Prozent der deutschen Erwerbstätigen kennen bereits solche Einsätze, in den USA sind es 25 und in den Niederlanden sogar über 26 Prozent.
- Small Office/Home Office (SOHO): Als Selbstständiger (z. B. Steuerberater, Anwalt, Pflegefachkraft) arbeitet man im häuslichen oder angemieteten Minibüro bzw. beim Kunden.
- Desk-Sharing: Zwei oder mehr Kollegen teilen sich einen Büroarbeitsplatz. Während der eine frei hat oder auf Dienstreise ist, kann der andere dort sitzen – und umgekehrt.
- Arbeitsplatz auf Rädern: Jeder Angestellte hat einen Rollcontainer mit seinen persönlichen Dingen und aktuellen Projektunterlagen, den er morgens an den ihm zugewiesenen Schreibtisch schiebt und abends wieder wegschließt.

Risiken und Nebenwirkungen

Obwohl in Deutschland große, meist internationale Unternehmen schon in der Zukunft angekommen sind und immer mehr Firmen folgen, gibt es auch Kritiker der neuen Arbeitswelt: Allzu flexible Bürokonzepte könnten die Beschäftigten ablenken und die Konzentration erschweren. Wo früher Zugehörigkeit und eine Art „Büro-Heimatgefühl" herrschten, läuft der moderne Angestellte Gefahr, zu einem Nomaden zu werden. Außerdem fürchtet so mancher Vorgesetze um seine Kontrollmöglichkeiten. Und viele Unternehmen scheuen die Investitionen in die nötige Computertechnologie oder sehen Sicherheitsrisiken beim Datentransfer, etwa von der Firmenzentrale zu einem Telearbeiter im heimischen Arbeitszimmer. „Den reinen Nomaden wird es daher ebenso wenig geben wie das seit Jahrzehnten propagierte papierlose Büro", ist sich Strese sicher.

12 Reminders

1 **The text below is about a Scottish couple who run a small business. Complete it with expressions from the box.**

> bills • cashflow • expensive • invoice • original terms of payment • owed to • receive • rely on • settled

Husband and wife team Debbie and Craig Stewart have run their own small business for seven years. They are based in the Scottish city of Inverness where they operate a fleet of 17 minibuses. They hire these out to hotels, conference centres and local companies for shuttle services and short business trips. Their company is called Tartan Shuttle Ltd. Like all SMEs, Debbie and Craig **(1)** rely on their clients to pay their **(2)** ______ promptly. Fuel is **(3)** ______ , the vehicles have to be cleaned and serviced, and they employ ten drivers. If they don't **(4)** ______ money which is **(5)** ______ them, it can quickly cause a **(6)** ______ problem. This morning, Debbie is discussing an **(7)** ______ with Craig. An American holiday company, which hired two of their minibuses in June, has not yet **(8)** ______ its account. Under the **(9)** ______ ______ , the company should have paid three weeks ago.

Invoice No.	74451/J
Amount	£5,450.00
Payment due	24 July
Payment received	£0.00
PAYMENT IS NOW OVERDUE	

2 ***Should have done / should have been done?*** **Complete the sentences with the correct active or passive forms of the verbs.**

1. **(pay)** The company should have paid three weeks ago.
2. **(make)** Payment should have been made last week.
3. **(settle)** They ______ ______ their account on 1 October.
4. **(receive)** You ______ ______ our invoice last Tuesday.
5. **(deliver)** The goods ______ ______ a week ago.
6. **(pay)** The bill ______ ______ promptly.
7. **(tell)** You ______ us about the problem immediately.
8. **(enclose)** A copy of the invoice ______ ______ with the letter.

Should have (done)

Should have stays the same in all persons:

	should	have	3. Form
I / we / you / he / they	should	have	paid

Ich / wir / Sie hätte(n) bezahlen sollen.

Passive

	should	have been	3. Form
The bill	should	have been	paid

… hätte bezahlt werden sollen.

3 **Below and on the next page are the main parts of reminder letters and replies to reminders. Complete the missing key English phrases.**

Writing a reminder

1. Ich schreibe Ihnen, weil …

I am writing ______ our invoice no. 1234	*mit Bezug auf*
______ payment is now overdue.	*Unseren Unterlagen entnehmen wir, dass …*

2. Entsprechend unseren vereinbarten Bedingungen …

______	*Entsprechend unseren vereinbarten Bedingungen …*
______ within 30 days.	*Zahlung sollte erfolgen (Anmerkung = hätte gemacht werden sollen)*

3. Eine Kopie unserer Rechnung …

I am enclosing a copy of the invoice ______	*für Ihre Unterlagen*

4. Dies ist wahrscheinlich ein Versehen (aber) …

This is probably a simple ______ …	*Dies ist wahrscheinlich ein Versehen*
I am sure you have mistakenly ______ this …	*Sie haben sicherlich übersehen*
… but we would be grateful if you could ______	*der Sache sofort nachgehen*
… but must ask you to ______	*in den nächsten Tagen, Ihr Konto auszugleichen.*

5. Zum Schluss

______, …	*Sollten Sie die Rechnung in der Zwischenzeit beglichen haben, …*
… please ______ this reminder and accept our thanks.	*als gegenstandslos betrachten*
______	*Wenn Sie Fragen bzw. Bedenken bezüglich der Zahlung haben, zögern Sie bitte nicht, sich mit uns in Verbindung zu setzen.*

Replying to a reminder → SB: S.115

1. Entschuldigung

Thank you for your letter ______ about our invoice no. 1234.	*vom 31. April*
We can only apologise for the ______	*Zahlungsverzug*

2. Die Ursache dafür ...
The delay is due to ...

... an oversight in our ______	*Buchhaltung(sabteilung)*
... the fact that we have a large number of employees who ______ at the moment.	*wegen Krankheit fehlen*
... a ______ problem with our cashflow.	*vorübergehend*
... a problem with one of our ______ who has not paid a bill.	*Kunden*

3. Zahlung erfolgt ...

Payment will be made immediately / within the next three days.

Wir wären Ihnen sehr dankbar, wenn ...
We would be extremely grateful if ...

... you could grant us a ______ of 30 days.	*Aufschub*
... you could arrange for us to pay ______	*in Raten*

4. Wir hoffen ...

We hope that you will ______ our (difficult) situation.	*Verständnis haben*
We look forward ______	*mit Ihnen weiterhin Geschäfte zu machen*

4 **Use the phrases from the diagrams to write reminder letters and the replies to reminders below. You need only write the text (without addresses etc.). Look in your book (pages 112, 113 and 115) and find other phrases that you can use also. Think of at least two more letters yourself.**

1. Write a reminder to the American holiday company for Mr and Mrs Stewart (page 63), then write a reply from the American company: it has a large number of employees who are off sick at the moment but they will pay immediately.
2. Ihre Firma stellt externe Festplatten *(external hard drives)* her und hat letzten Monat 2.000 Platten an einen britischen Großhändler geliefert (Ansprechpartner Robert Gardner); vereinbarte Bedingungen: Zahlung innerhalb von 30 Tagen; Zahlung steht jetzt seit 21 Tagen aus. Bitte um Ausgleich in den nächsten Tagen. **Antwort:** Problem liegt an einem Kunden, der sein Konto nicht ausgeglichen hat. Bitte um Aufschub von 30 Tagen.
3. Die Marketingagentur für die Sie arbeiten hat neulich in Deutschland für eine amerikanische Firma eine Marktanalyse durchgeführt. Bedingungen: Zahlung innerhalb von 60 Tagen. Zahlung steht jetzt aus; Firma hat bis jetzt immer pünktlich bezahlt. **Antwort:** vorübergehende Cashflow-Probleme. Bitte um Möglichkeit, in Raten zu zahlen.

5 EXTRA **Your German boss would like information about the law in the EU about late payment and some tips for how to deal with customers who pay late. Make notes in German for her from the text in your book on page 113 ('What the law says about late payment').**

6 ROUNDUP **Write the correct word (a, b or c) in each sentence.**

1. Late payment is when a company which has received goods or services doesn't ______ its account promptly.
   a pay
   b send
   c settle
2. Promptly means 'according to the ______ terms at the time of sale'.
   a agreed
   b understood
   c decided.
3. When writing a reminder letter, it's always a good idea to enclose a copy of the original invoice for the customer's ______ .
   a convenience
   b convenient
   c conveniently
4. It's also usual to offer the customer an explanation – i.e. say something like: 'You have probably ______ overlooked this'.
   a mistake
   b mistook
   c mistakenly
5. You should certainly always say that if the customer has already paid the invoice in the meantime, they should ______ your reminder.
   a deal with
   b accept
   c disregard
6. Be 'polite but firm' in your letter – so finish with a phrase like: 'We look forward to ______ from you very soon.
   a receive payment
   b receiving payment
   c making payment
7. In many cases, there is in fact a good explanation for late payment – even if it's just administrative ______ .
   a debt
   b inefficiency
   c intentional
8. A common problem is that your customer has its own problem with one of its customers who hasn't paid them. In that case, they may ask for an ______ – i.e. the chance to pay later.
   a instalment
   b expansion
   c extension

13 Industry, service and trade (2)

A Young experts talking

→ SB: S.116–117

1 **Finish this report on the tourist industry in Barbados last year with expressions from the box.**

accommodation • average temperatures • beaches • coral • destination • generated • income • located • market • scuba diving • seasons • tourist arrivals

Barbados: Tourist Industry Statistics

Background

Barbados is an independent island nation (1) located in the Eastern Caribbean. With a total land area of only 430 square kilometres, it is extremely small for a Caribbean island. Nevertheless, it has a high standard of living (last year it was ranked 31st in the world and third in the Americas after the USA and Canada).

Tourism in Barbados

With sandy (2) ______________, (3) ______________ reefs, world-class (4) ______________, and excellent hotels, it is not surprising that Barbados is a popular tourist (5) ______________ and that tourism is a major industry on the island. Last year, (6) ______________ from tourism made up 12.4% of the island's GDP.

Tourism statistics

- Total (7) ______________ in Barbados last year were 1,272,772, an increase of almost 16% over the previous year.
- Direct and indirect spending on tourism (8) ______________ US$579 million.
- There is no large difference between the (9) ______________ when it comes to the number of visits. Winter has the slightly larger number of visits (51.3%). This is because (10) ______________ stay between 27 and 32 °C all year round, so that from October to March, Barbados offers a break from the cold weather in other countries.
- The average length of stay on the island is 6.8 nights. Rented apartments are the most popular form of (11) ______________ (54%) followed by hotels (42%) and guest houses (2.5%).
- With its history as part of the British Commonwealth and because English is the national language of Barbados, it is also no suprise that Barbados's biggest single tourist (12) ______________ is the UK (38.8%) Important numbers of visitors also come from the USA, Canada, and the Caricom (Caribbean Community) area – other countries in the Caribbean region.

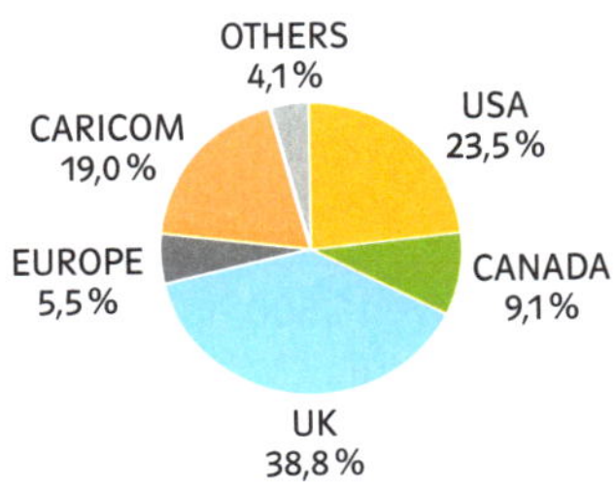

2 EXTRA **Translate the report into German.**

B Language toolbox: Reporting what people have said

→ SB: S.118–119, GS: E

1 **Stephanie Wittmar works in the marketing department of a German holiday company called Germany By Bike – GBB. She's in Britain this week to promote *(für etwas werben)* her company. Yesterday she gave a presentation at the head office of a large chain of travel agents. What did she say? Finish the sentences below and on page 69.**

1. GBB is seven years old. It's based in Berlin.

Stephanie said GBB was seven years old. It was based in Berlin.

2. The company specialises in cycling holidays for younger people.

She said ______

3. Holidays last between four and nine days. People travel in groups of about ten.

She told the audience that ______

4. GBB arranges accommodation each night and transports people's luggage.

She explained that ______

5. Last year, GBB arranged over 1,500 holiday tours. All were very successful.

Stephanie told her listeners that ______

6. In August last year, a well-known German travel magazine gave GBB an award *(Preis)* for Best Customer Service By A Small Company.

She mentioned that ______

7. The market in Germany for cycling holidays is growing constantly.

______

8. Cycling holidays are becoming more and more popular.

______

9. In the last five years, the market has grown by almost 70%.

10. It will certainly grow more in the future.

11. GBB will continue to be a major player in the industry.

12. British cyclists would love cycling in Germany.

2 **After Stephanie's presentation, a secretary at the British travel agency wrote up the minutes. Below, you can see an extract from them. What were Stephanie's original words?**

1. Ms Wittmar said that GBB offered a range of holidays in different locations. Among others, there were tours of Bavaria, the Black Forest, the River Rhine and Germany's capital city, Berlin. Two years ago, it had also started offering tours in Thuringia.
2. She explained that because the target group was younger people, accommodation was usually in guest houses or cheaper hotels. The typical cost of a 7-day tour was around 400 euros. That included accommodation, food, and hire of the cycles and cycling equipment. Travel to and from Germany itself was not included in the price.
3. Ms Wittmar told the agency that for new customers, GBB would offer a discount of 10% on all holidays for the first six months. It would also provide sales brochures in English.

Stephanie: GBB offers a range of holidays in different locations. Among others, there

D Business topics: Ethical holidays

→ SB: S.122–123

1 **The sentences in the table show *how* certain things are being done or can be done. Match the questions 1–4 and the solutions a–d.**

QUESTIONS		SOLUTIONS	
1	How are travel companies meeting customer demand for ethical holidays?	a	You can pay a little extra when you book a ticket.
2	How are some responsible tourists trying to reduce the impact of their holidays on the environment?	b	They can employee people from their area and use local food.
3	How can you offset your carbon emissions when you fly?	c	They're developing innovative solutions to holidays.
4	How can hotels make sure that the local community benefits from tourism?	d	They're staying at home or travelling by train instead of by plane.

1 ___ 2 ___ 3 ___ 4 ___

► **meet the demand for sthg** *den Bedarf für etwas decken*

2 **Now look at the box and write three sentences with the information from the table and *by*.**

→ GS: D6 (4)

1. Travel companies are meeting customer demand for ethical holidays by developing ___
2. ___
3. ___

By doing

You can explain *how* things are done with the useful expression **by + -ing-Form** *(indem …)*:

Flying has a big effect on the environment. People can reduce CO_2 pollution ***by travelling*** *by train instead of by plane.*

How can hotels play their part in eco-friendly tourism? One way they can do that is ***by using*** *energy-saving electrical appliances*

3 **Answer these questions about ethical holidays with a sentence with *by*. Write on a separate piece of paper.**

1. Big hotel chains can play their part in eco-friendly tourism by using energy-saving electrical equipment. How can they be eco-friendly in two other ways?
   They can also be eco-friendly by … and by …
2. How is CBT (Community Based Tourism) helping tourists to understand other cultures better?
3. How is one CBT project in the Amazon helping local people?
4. How can you find out about ethical holidays?

4 EXTRA **Can you write sentences with *by* about these general business topics? Write on a separate piece of paper again.**

1. How do companies usually make sure that people know about their products?
2. Companies often transport goods by road, but road transport pollutes the environment. How could companies reduce the impact of transport on the environment?
3. Suppliers always want to attract new B2B customers. How can they do this when they write an offer letter to a potential customer?

Now you. Write a sentence yourself about another business topic.

Video lounge

→ SB: S.125, Schüler DVD V5, Schüler DVD Transkript

1 **Before you watch the video, look through the background information and the useful expressions below.**

The counties of Devon and Cornwall are two of England's most popular tourist regions. Carlyon Bay is a seaside resort in Cornwall.

Hadley Centre for Climate Prediction
A UK government organisation that studies how global warming is affecting the UK.

'Planning struggles'
A company that wants to build for example a new hotel must first get planning permission *(Baugenehmigung)*. Sometimes there are vigorous objections *(gravierende Einsprüche)* and that can lead to a struggle *(Kampf)*. If the problem is really bad, there can be a public enquiry *(öffentliche Untersuchung)*. It will look at both sides and pass judgement *(ein Urteil sprechen)*.

Useful expressions

scorcher *sehr heißer Tag*
lure *Verlockung*
devise *ausarbeiten, formulieren*
set (to change) *(hier) wird sich bald ändern*
influx *Einströmen*
prediction *Voraussage*
picture (v.) *(hier) Stellen Sie sich … vor*
spring up *(plötzlich) erscheinen*
prospect *Aussicht*
cope (with sth.) *(etw.) bewältigen*
clogged *verkehrsreich, verstopft*
put strain on sthg. *etw. belasten*
waste *(hier) Abfallentsorgung*
relentless *unablässig*

2 **Watch the video once all through to get a general idea. Then watch again in sections.**

Section 1: 'Turning up the heat'

1. The BBC reporter that you hear is David Shukman. What does he want us to imagine in the first part of the clip?
2. Mr Shukman interviews a scientist called David Viner. What does Mr Viner explain? What does he say this will mean in the future?

Section 2: Changes to the British coastline

3. Mr Shukman explains that 'if (David Viner's) predictions are correct, the British coastline faces dramatic change as millions of people head (= come) here for their holidays.' What will those changes be? What question does Mr Shukman ask about the changes?
4. He then interviews two people from Carlyon Bay: a man in a pub and a lady in the street. What do they think about new developments in their town?

Section 3: Interview with a Cornish tourism expert

5. David Shukman interviews a tourism expert from Cornwall.
   a) What does she say at the beginning that is positive about new developments?
   b) She also talks about the 'downside'. What does she say?

Section 4: Ending the report

6. Who, according to Mr Shukman, will be the 'winners and losers' in Mediterranean Britain?
7. What does he say could 'now spring up here'?

3 **What are the advantages and disadvantages of tourism in a town or city? What decisions do people there have to make about how they want tourism to develop in their area? Write about your ideas on a separate piece of paper.**

E Be an English expert!: Prepositions

→ SB: S. 126

1 **Practise using prepositions by completing these sentences.**

1. I'm very interested in sport but I'm not so keen ________ music.
2. Herr Schenk is responsible ________ sales in our company.
3. A management assistant has to be good ________ English.
4. Their new product is very similar ________ a product we make.
5. This food is typical ________ the sorts of things we eat in this country.
6. I'm afraid I don't agree ________ Jack about this.
7. The company specialises ________ ethical holidays.
8. We may buy it or we may not. It depends ________ the price.
9. You can divide a market ________ a number of segments.
10. So who is going to pay ________ transporting the goods?
11. The town has spent a lot of money ________ new hotels.
12. Do you have the details ________ Mr Long's trip next week?
13. The percentage ________ people who travel abroad for their holidays has risen.
14. This is a good example ________ German efficiency!
15. The main reason ________ growth in this area is that people have more disposable income.
16. That isn't a good idea ________ my opinion.
17. I think you have sent us the wrong goods ________ mistake.
18. Ms Nelson's office is ________ the third floor.
19. Sales this year have been good - ________ contrast to sales last year, which were bad.
20. Do you travel much ________ business?
21. Dave isn't in the office this week. He's ________ holiday.
22. ________ conclusion, I would like to thank you for inviting me here today.
23. I heard an excellent programme ________ the radio last week.
24. They sell a lot of unusual products ________ addition to the ones you usually find.

2 EXTRA **Practise your mediation skills. The text below is from a report about tourism in Germany in the first seven months of this year. Make notes on the important points in English.**

Urlaub in Deutschland

Deutschland, als Ferienziel, lag auch in diesem Sommer im Trend. Klassische Ferienregionen wie die schleswig-holsteinische Nordseeküste, Ostfriesland, der Westerwald, der Schwarzwald und der Bodensee verzeichneten Zuwächse. Dagegen mussten insbesondere die Destinationen in Mecklenburg-Vorpommern wegen des Wetters und aufgrund des verschärften Wettbewerbs mit dem Nachbarland Polen in dieser Saison Verluste hinnehmen. Gewinner sind wieder einmal die Städte. In den ersten sieben Monaten des Jahres wurden vom Statistischen Bundesamt bundesweit rund ein Drittel aller Gäste (23,4 Millionen von insgesamt 67,9 Millionen Gästen) in Städten mit mehr als 100.000 Einwohnern gezählt. Die Besucher erzeugten in den Großstädten 45,7 Millionen Übernachtungen (plus 5,2 Prozent). Besonders beliebt sind die deutschen Metropolen, vor allem jene, die von Low-Cost-Carriern angeflogen werden. So verbuchte etwa Dresden bei den Übernachtungen in den ersten sieben Monaten ein Plus von 11,9 Prozent, Köln 11,6 Prozent, Berlin 9,2 Prozent. Die positive Entwicklung lässt sich auf eine steigende Zahl von Kurzurlauben, Geschäfts- und Eventreisen zurückführen.

14 Taking messages

1 **Saba Schabani is a management assistant at Arndorfer GmbH, a German import company based in Dusseldorf. Her boss Frau Lütkemeyer is away on a business trip this week and Saba is taking phone messages for her. Complete her conversation with a Japanese businessman with phrases from the box.**

> 81-3-4455-3131 • And can I just take your phone number, please? • And could you give me the company name again • And your message is • Can I just check that I've got everything correct? • Can I take a message? • Could I take your name again? • I'll make sure Mrs Lütkemeyer gets your message as soon as she's back in the office. • ~~I'm sorry~~ • She's away all week. • You're welcome.

Saba Arndorfer Imports. Schabani. Guten Tag.
Caller Hello. Could I speak to Mrs Lütkemeyer, please?
Saba (1) I'm sorry, she's away on a business trip at the moment. (2) ____________
Caller When will she be back?
Saba Not until next Monday. (3) ____________
Caller I see. OK. This is Yukio Takashi from the Konoshima Corporation in Tokyo, Japan. Could you tell Mrs Lütkemeyer that I'm coming to Germany next month and I'd like to meet her? I'll call back next week to arrange a date.
Saba (4) ____________
Caller It's Yukio, that's Y-U-K-I-O, Takashi, T-A-K-A-S-H-I.
Saba (5) ____________, Mr Takashi?
Caller Sure. The Konoshima Corporation. K-O-N-O-S-H-I-M-A Corporation.
Saba (6) ____________
Caller It's 81 for Japan, then 3-double 4 double 5, 3131.
Saba (7) ____________
Caller Right.
Saba (8) ____________: You are coming to Germany next month and you would like to meet Mrs Lütkemeyer. You'll call back next week to arrange a date.
Caller Exactly.
Saba (9) ____________ Mr Yukio Takashi, from the Konoshima Corporation in Tokyo. Telephone number 81-3-4455-3131. I've written: 'Mr Takashi is coming to Germany next week and would like to meet you. He'll call back next week to arrange a date.'
Caller That's all correct.
Saba Thank you for your patience Mr Takashi. (10) ____________
Caller Thank you very much for your help.
Saba (11) ____________ Bye now.
Caller Goodbye.

2 Now YOU. Your boss Carsten Wimmer is out of the office today and you're taking telephone messages from callers. Look at the example then write the other messages below. (You can copy the Telephone Message form if you want).

Telephone Message

To Herr Wimmer

Date 12 March

Time 11.45

Caller Mr Kevin Farelly

Company Bostelex Inc

Phone number 617 712-0645

Message Mr Farelly enjoyed his visit to us last week and would like to say 'thank you' again for all your hospitality. He's looking forward to your visit to the U.S. in May.

Taken by (Your name)

1. "This is Sangeet Sharma from New Delhi Engineering Ltd."
"My phone number is 11-6923345."
"Could you tell Mr Wimmer that I need to speak to him urgently about the delivery of some goods? I'll call back at 9 o'clock your time tomorrow morning."

2. "This is Jack Rogers from the National Exhibition Centre in Birmingham, England."
"Our phone number is 44 for the UK then 121 780-4141."
"Could you ask Mr Wimmer to send me all the details of his stand at the trade fair next month, please? I need the information fairly quickly if possible."

3. "This is Margareta Halvorsen from Stanqvist AB in Kristianstad, Sweden."
"My telephone number is 044 10 13 66."
"Could you tell Mr Wimmer, please, that I have to cancel our meeting on 4 April? I apologise for this but something important has come up. Could ask him to let me have some dates when he's free so we can arrange another meeting?"

4. "This is Mark Gilbert from the First Oklahoma Bank."
"Mr Wimmer has my number."
"Could you let Mr Wimmer know that everything is arranged for next month? Our two representatives will meet him in New York on the 23rd. I've also got some tickets for a New York Mets baseball game!"

How messages work

Remember that messages can give information or be a request:

- *Could you tell Mr Wimmer that …* **(giving information)**
- *Could you ask Mr Wimmer to send me …* **(request)**.

Check in your book on page 131 how you write the two sorts of telephone messages.

3 You have another call for your boss Mr Wimmer. Use the diagram below to write the complete conversation in English. Write on a separate piece of paper.

	YOU	CALLER
1.	Melden Sie sich (Ihre Firma ist die Eschler GmbH).	"Ich hätte gern mit Herrn Wimmer gesprochen."
2.	Erklären Sie, dass er heute nicht im Büro ist und fragen Sie, ob Sie etwas ausrichten können.	"Wann kommt er wieder?"
3.	Sagen Sie, dass Herr Wimmer erst morgen wieder kommt.	"OK. Hier spricht Martin Rutherford von UK Wholesale Ltd in London. Bitte sagen Sie Herrn Wimmer, dass ich übernächste Woche in Düsseldorf bin und dass ich ihn gerne treffen würde. Ich rufe Anfang nächster Woche an, um einen Termin auszumachen."
4.	Bitten Sie den Anrufer nochmals um seinen Namen.	"Rutherford. Martin Rutherford."
5.	Fragen Sie ob er seinen Namen bitte buchstabieren könnte.	"Sicher. Martin, M-A-R-T-I-N, Rutherford, R-U-T-H-E-R-F-O-R-D."
6.	Bitten Sie Herrn Rutherford um seine Telefonnummer.	"Meine Nummer ist: 020 246 4286."
7.	Wiederholen Sie kurz die Nachricht.	"Ja, das ist richtig."
8.	Bestätigen Sie noch einmal alle Daten und die Nachricht (wie Sie sie für Ihren Chef notiert haben).	"Klasse."
9.	Sie werden Herrn Wimmer Bescheid sagen.	"Danke für Ihre Hilfe. Auf Wiederhören."
10	Nichts zu Danken. Verabschieden Sie sich.	

4 EXTRA **Practise using the international telephone alphabet. Write the names using Alpha, Bravo, Charlie etc.** → SB: S.79

1. Wolfgang Whisky - Oscar - Lima - Foxtrot - Golf - Alpha - November - Golf
2. Schmidt ______
3. Koeln ______
4. Zimmermann ______

Now write your name and some companies you know using the international alphabet.

5 ROUNDUP **Which is the correct word – a, b or c?**

1. She isn't here ______ the moment.
   a) in b) on c) at
2. May I ______ your name, please?
   a) write b) call c) take
3. How do you ______ your name?
   a) spell b) write c) give
4. Sorry, I didn't quite ______ that.
   a) hear b) learn c) catch
5. ______ give you the number again just in case.
   a) I better b) I'll better c) I'd better
6. I'll ______ he gets the message.
   a) look b) see c) watch
7. Can I make a ______ of your number?
   a) note b) notice c) notes
8. I'll ring again ______.
   a) other time b) more times c) another time
9. Mr Smith will ______ your call as soon as he gets back.
   a) return b) confirm c) repeat
10. ______ is Fred Jones from ABC Ltd.
    a) Here b) Speaking c) This

15 Challenges of a global economy

A World experts talking

→ SB: S.134–135
(Vgl. WB S.12 EU nationalities)

1 EXTRA **Here are some nationalities from around the world. Complete the sentences below.**

Country/Continent	Adjective	Person	Population (people)
1 -*(i)an*			
Africa	African	an African	the Africans
the Amazon (region)	Amazonian	an Amazonian	the Amazonians
America	American	an American	the Americans
Asia	Asian	an Asian	the Asians
Australia	Australian	an Australian	the Australians
Brazil	Brazilian	a Brazilian	the Brazilians
Cambodia	Cambodia	a Cambodian	the Cambodians
Canada	Canadian	a Canadian	the Canadians
Egypt	Egyptian	an Egyptian	the Egyptians
Europe	European	a European	the Europeans
India	Indian	an Indian	the Indians
Indonesia	Indonesian	an Indonesian	the Indonesians
Kenya	Kenyan	a Kenyan	the Kenyans
Mexico	Mexican	a Mexican	the Mexicans
Morocco	Moroccan	a Moroccan	the Moroccans
Russia	Russian	a Russian	the Russians
Uganda	Ugandan	a Ugandan	the Ugandans
2 -*ese*			
China	Chinese	a Chinese	the Chinese
Japan	Japanese	a Japanese	the Japanese
Vietnam	Vietnamese	a Vietnamese	the Vietnamese
Lebanon	Lebanese	a Lebanese	the Lebanese
3 -*i*			
Iraq	Iraqui	an Iraqui	the Iraquis
Israel	Israeli	an Israeli	the Israelis
Saudi Arabia	Saudi	a Saudi	the Saudis
Thailand	Thai	a Thai	the Thais
Pakistan	Pakistani	a Pakistani	the Pakistanis

1. There are eight people in your book on pages 134 to 135. Vance Mueller is from North America; he's an American. Ina is from Europe; she's a ______. Parvati is from India; she's an ______. Ming is from China; he's a ______. Seng Chanlina comes from Cambodia; she's a ______. Leopold comes from Uganda; he's a ______. Payakan is from the Amazon; he's an ______. And Todd is another ______.
2. The capital of Japan is Tokyo. It's the ______ capital.
3. Japan has a very old and traditional culture. People sometimes say the ______ are not easy to understand.
4. A lot of Brazil is covered by rainforest. The ______ rainforest is gigantic.
5. My friend comes from Thailand. He's a ______. He lives in the ______ capital Bangkok.
6. Kenya and Uganda were once part of the British Commonwealth and the ______ and the ______ still use English as an official language *(Amtssprache)*.
7. We do a lot of business with Pakistan. One of our biggest customers is a ______ company based in Islamabad.
8. Winter sports are popular in Lebanon. There are six major ______ ski resorts, all world class.

B Language toolbox: Asking for and giving information

1 **German businesswoman Astrid Schleusner is a regular business traveller. Her company has a number of business partners in Asia. Help Astrid to make polite questions that she can use when she's flying, staying at hotels, and taking part in meetings.**

1. Where do I check in for the flight to Tokyo?
   Could you tell me where I check in for the flight to Tokyo, please?
2. Is the plane to Bangkok on time?
3. Where can I get a taxi?
4. What time is breakfast?
5. How do I phone Germany from my hotel room?
6. Do you have internet access in all the rooms?
7. Is there a good restaurant near here?
8. Is your office in the city centre?
9. What is Mr Tanaka's cell phone number?
10. Where are the women's toilets?
11. How big is your product range?
12. When are you visiting Germany?

Polite questions

A polite question is a way to ask a 'normal' question indirectly and so more politely. Polite questions normally begin with *Could you tell me/us …* and end with *please?* You can make them with a question word *(when, what time, where)* or *if* (= 'ob'). **Notice the word order!**

	When	*is the next train?*
Could you tell me	*when*	*the next train is, please?*
	Where	*do I check in?*
Could you tell me	*where*	*I check in, please?*
	Is Mr Jones here?	
Could you tell me	*if Mr Jones is here, please?*	

2 **Finish the sentences with forms of *think* or *mean*.**

1. Sorry, Mr Wong. I don't quite understand what you _mean_.
2. We have to make a decision. James, what do you ______________ about this?
3. James: I ______________ it was a good idea at first. But now I ______________ (not) we should do business with them. It's too risky.
4. The word 'challenge' ______________ 'Herausforderung' in German.
5. Lots of things have happened in the last 50 years and that has ______________ huge changes in people's lives.

Think* and *mean

The verbs *think* and *mean* are used differently in English.

mean
- heißen: *What does 'turnover' mean? It means 'Umsatz'.*
- bedeuten / zur Folge haben: *The economic crisis means that lots of people will become unemployed.*
- sagen wollen: *What do you mean? – I mean / I'm trying to say that …*

think
- der Meinung sein: *I think that's terrible!*

Business topics: Sweatshops

→ SB: S. 140 – 141

1 **Words to express your opinions and feelings. Which words below can you use to express a positive opinion and which are negative? Write two lists. (TIP: There are more negative words than positive words). Use your dictionary if you're not sure of the meanings.**

~~(quite) acceptable~~ • appalling • awful / terrible • brilliant *(informal)* • crazy / stupid *(informal)* • depressing • disappointing • disgusting • encouraging • excellent • ridiculous • sad • strange / odd • surprising • unacceptable • unbelievable • understandable • wonderful

POSITIVE

(quite) acceptable

NEGATIVE

2 **Now use words from the boxes to express your opinions about these facts from the text about sweatshops on pages 140 – 141 of your book.**

1. "A famous model who modelled the clothes (made in a sweatshop) earned more in one day than a worker would earn in 4,000 years." (Lines 11 – 12)

   I think it's ridiculous / I find it ridiculous that a model in Europe or the USA can earn more in just one day than a sweatshop worker would earn in 4,000 years.

2. "Relatively speaking, clothes in our shops (in Europe) are cheaper now than ever before." (Introduction)

   ____

3. "Jivaj works around 12 hours a day, but sometimes (…) it's more." (Lines 37–39)

4. "It is true that things have certainly improved." (Line 54)

5. "It's almost impossible to track down all of these terrible sweatshops." (Lines 59–60)

6. All businesses try to make the biggest possible profit. (Not directly in the text but generally true)

- Choose four or five more facts from the text about sweatshops and write sentences giving your opinion. Write on a separate piece of paper.

3 **Answer these questions about the interview with Neil Wincroft. Before beginning, look back at the earlier pages in your workbook shown below. Practise using the expressions you learned there again here. Write on a separate piece of paper.**

→ Hörtexte Transkript

1. What does 'fundraising' mean exactly?
   Fundraising basically means raising money for the organisation with campaigns, sponsorship etc.
2. How was the Fairtrade organisation formed? (TIP: *by* + combining)
3. What is the (main) idea behind the Fairtrade organisation?
4. What is the (main) reason why the organisation is necessary in today's global world?
5. What exactly is a 'stable price' and why is it important?
6. How does Fairtrade help farmers in the Developing World? (TIP: two ways: (a) finding partners in Europe; (b) guaranteeing prices)
7. Is there a (small) downside for consumers here who buy Fairtrade goods? Is that a really big problem? Explain.
8. What is the 'Fairtrade mark'?
9. Why is the mark important? Give two reasons?
10. Who checks that the mark is valid? What is the advantage of that system?

Interview Neil Wincroft, Fairtraide

Page 37
It's a kind / sort / type of …

Page 38: Giving reasons
because …
because of …
The main / Another reason why … is that …

Page 50: pros and cons
The big advantage of … is that …
The downside is that …

Page 60: Explaining
X basically means that …
Another word for X is …

Page 70: *By doing* (indem)
You can do X by doing Y.

Video lounge

→ SB: S.143, Schüler DVD V6, Schüler DVD Transkript

1 Before you watch the video, look through the expressions below.

stagnation (economics) *(Wirtschafts)Flaute*
belt *(hier) Region*
barely *kaum*
poverty *Armut*
eradicate *ausrotten*
set out *sich auf den Weg machen*
machete *Machete (Buschmesser)*
hack (oneself) *(sich) hacken*

2 Now watch and make notes in the diagram below.

Economic reasons for child labour in the Ivory Coast

The 'Cocoa Protocol' – When? Why? Who?

Marc's father and life in Marc's village

Marc's story

The BBC reporter's questions to the viewers at the end

3 Write a summary in English of the video. Begin like this:

In this video called 'Cocoa Children' a reporter from the BBC visits the Ivory Coast, the West African country which supplies half the world's cocoa. He wants to find out about ...

E Be an English expert!

1 Try this 'phrasal verbs' crossword. It is more difficult than the other crosswords!

Note:

- all the verbs are written as one word: *cut down* = CUTDOWN
- The verbs can be in different tenses: FOUNDOUT / TOOKOFF

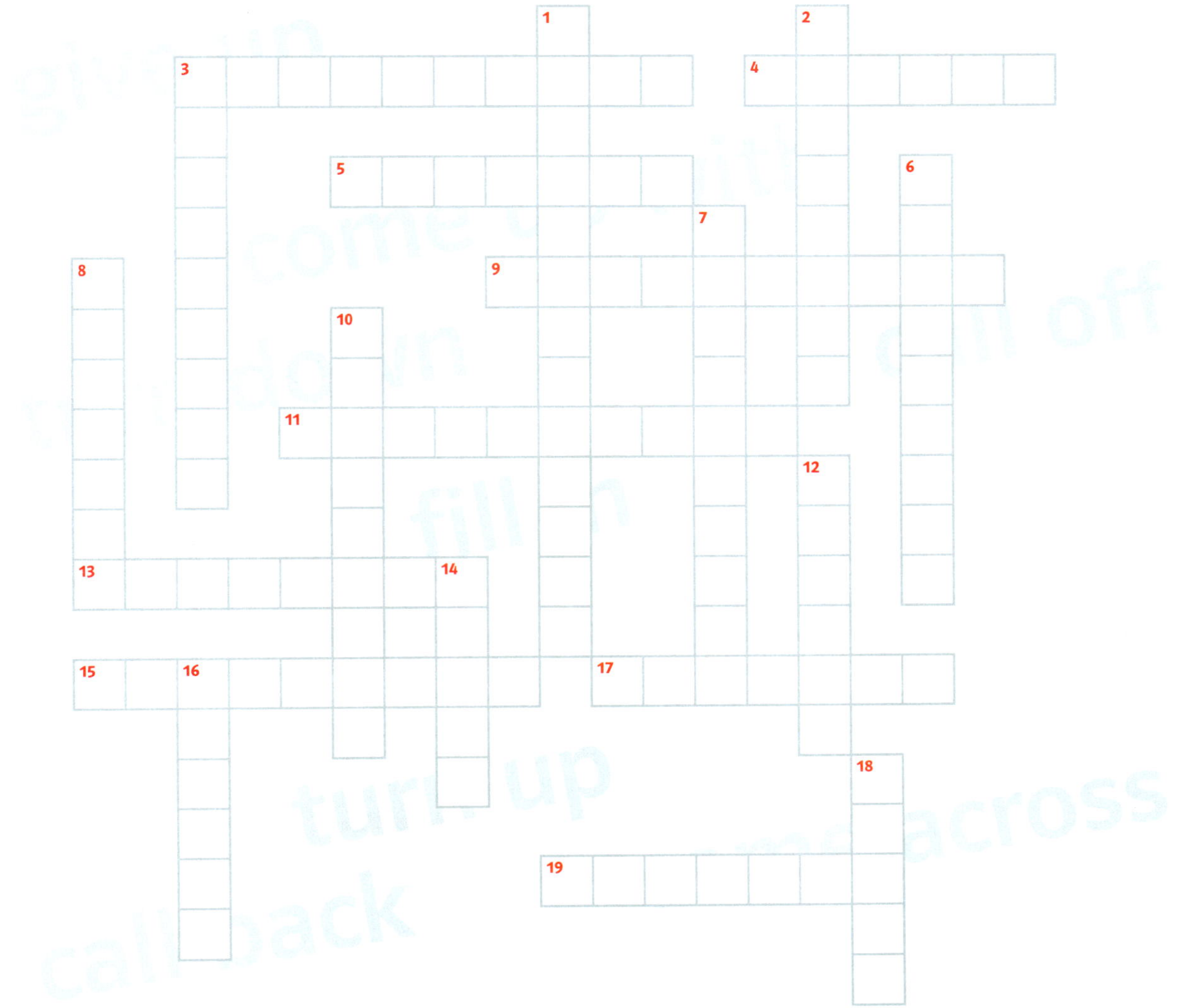

DOWN

1 Thank you again for your enquiry. We ... receiving your order soon.

2 To advertise their new product, they ... lots of free samples. People paid nothing for them.

3 Ms Ewert cancelled the meeting last week. She ... the meeting.

6 Next week I'm starting a new job. I hope I ... my new colleagues!

7 The firm decided not to buy our products. They ... our offer.

8 My office is a mess! I really must ... my papers.

10 I arrived late yesterday because my car ... on the way to the meeting.

12 I was just leaving the hotel, when the receptionist shouted: "... , please, sir. There's a phone call for you."

14 Our goods are too cheap. We should ... the price.

16 I used to get very stressed until I ... yoga.

18 Werner von Siemens ... his first company in 1847.

ACROSS

3 In the Cocoa Children video, the reporters ... Marc and his brother unexpectedly in the bush.

4 If the situation doesn't improve, I'm afraid we'll have to ... some of our workers.

5 What you do when you first arrive at an airport.

9 The product isn't selling as well as we hoped. We need to ... a really good advertising idea.

11 Anja is responsible for sales. She ... sales.

13 One of their sales representatives ... at our office yesterday. He didn't have an appointment.

15 We shouldn't just ... situations in the world that are unfair. We should try to do something.

17 I don't know the answer, but I'll try to ... for you.

19 Teacher to student in class: "Would you ... these handouts, please, Dirk?"

16 Commerce in action (revision)

Getting ready for your exam

In your exam*, you will have to write one of the commercial letters or emails you have learned about during your course: an enquiry, an offer, an order (possibly with an order form), a complaint or a reminder. You will be able to use a dictionary but you won't have access to the lists of phrases in your book. That means that you can look up unknown words (e.g. for a product) but you must know the phrases themselves. In most cases, you will be given a list of things to include in your letter. These will normally be in German.

*** Important! Check this information with your teacher. Not all exams will be the same.**

In this unit of the workbook you will find a typical exam task for each type of letter. Use it to practise writing. Use your dictionary, but *don't* look in your student's book for phrases. Check your answers afterwards in the key, correct your mistakes, and learn again the phrases you are not sure of.

1 A letter of enquiry

SITUATION
Reincom GmbH is a medium-sized German company which manufactures road sweeping vehicles. With 45 years' experience in the industry, the company has a good reputation for the quality of its products and its after sales customer service. It operates throughout Germany, Austria and since 2004 in Slovakia and Romania. Its head office address is: Kruppstraße 20-24, 52062 Aachen, Germany.

► **road sweeping vehicle** *Kehrfahrzeug*

PRODUKTION (Schriftlich)
Jacqueline Kamann works as a management assistant in Reincom's purchasing department. At a recent trade fair in Brussels, Jacqueline's boss Marcel Geißler, Reincom's purchasing manager, was interested in the products of a Belgian company which manufactures environmentally friendly brushes for use in the cleaning industry. The company's name and address is: Ecobrosse S.A., Bd de Lauzelle 56, 1348 Louvain-La-Neuve, Belgium. Herr Geißler asks Jacqueline to write a letter of enquiry to the company.

► **brush** *Kehrbesen*

YOUR TASK
On the right you can see Jacqueline's notes. Write a letter of enquiry. Use the correct letter layout. Write on a separate piece of paper.

- Produkte neulich auf der Cleaning Industry Exhibition in Brüssel gesehen
- wir sind ein mittelständischer Produzent von Kehrfahrzeugen in Deutschland und für hohe Qualität bekannt. (Weiteres auf unserer Website www.reincom.de)
- sind immer an neuen, umweltfreundlichen Produkten interessiert
- bitte Informationsmaterialien und Preisliste zuschicken
- Infos über Rabatte / Lieferzeiten würden uns auch interessieren
- angemessenes Briefende

2 An offer

SITUATION
Weingut Ardinger GmbH is a German wine producer that regularly wins international prizes for its wines. The vinyard, which is near Stuttgart, offers a wine range of wines from white to red, rosé and sparkling ('Sekt'). Founded in 1492, the business is an SME employing 37 people and is run by the Ardinger family. Its business address: Marktstraße 11, 71672 Marbach am Neckar, Germany.

PRODUKTION (Schriftlich)
Arno Mechling is a management assistant in the company's export sales department. His boss is Marion Ardinger. At the end of last week, Arno's department received an enquiry from a gourmet London restaurant, Le Walrus Vert, 21 Monmouth Street, London WC2H 9DD. Frau Ardinger wants Arno to write an offer letter and gives him the notes below.

YOUR TASK
Write the letter.

Herrn Dover vom Walrus Vert in London folgendes Angebot machen:

- danke für Ihren Brief (Datum usw.)
- anbei die aktuelle Preisliste
- alle Preise CIF Harwich. (Wir ziehen vor, unsere Weine per Binnenwasserstraße / Seetransport zu schicken, da kostengünstig und umweltfreundlich)
- Mengenrabatt von 5% auf Bestellungen über EUR 5.000
- beim ersten Auftrag wird die Bezahlung bei Auftragserteilung verlangt
- Lieferung erfolgt innerhalb von 14 Tagen nach Erhalt der Bestellung
- dieses Angebot ist 6 Monate gültig
- danke nochmals für Ihr Interesse an unseren Produkten
- wir sind uns sicher, dass Sie mit der Qualität unserer Weine sehr zufrieden sein werden
- sollten Sie weitere Fragen haben, zögern Sie bitte nicht usw.
- angemessenes Briefende

3 An order

SITUATION

The Hotel Königshof is a three-star hotel in Frankfurt. Within five minutes' walk of the central railway station (the address is Taunusstraße 70, 60311 Frankfurt/Main) the hotel is popular with business travellers. Breakfast is served in the morning in the restaurant. It is a buffet with fresh rolls, butter, a selection of jams, cold meat, cheese, fruit, joghurt, fruit juice, eggs, warm sausages and bacon, and tea or coffee to drink.

PRODUKTION (Schriftlich)

The hotel received an offer two weeks ago from a British jam manufacturer, Thurgood and Sons Ltd., Tiptree, CO5 0RF, England. You work as a management assistant at the hotel and the hotel manager, Karin Zipprich, wants you to place an order. She has filled out a purchase order (number 4422) and asks you to write a cover letter to send with the order form. She gives you the notes below.

YOUR TASK

Write the cover letter.

Bitte an Sophie Ellis (Export Managerin bei Thurgood) einen Begleitbrief schreiben.

- Danke für Ihr Angebot sowie die Muster, die Sie uns geschickt haben
- sind mit der Qualität der Produkte zufrieden
- beigefügt erhalten Sie unseren Auftrag (Nummer ...)
- wir bestätigen: alle Preise DDP Frankfurt / Einführungsrabatt von 10% / Zahlung innerhalb von 30 Tagen nach Erhalt der Bestellung / Lieferung innerhalb von 7 Tagen
- freuen uns auf rechtzeitiges Eintreffen der Ware und auf weitere Geschäfte mit Ihnen
- angemessenes Briefende

4 A complaint

SITUATION

Lifestyle 21 is a furniture store in Munich. The store opened five years ago and since then it has established a good reputation for quality. Many of its products are in the expensive, premium range. Furniture is bought for the store from around the world and generally speaking, the store enjoys excellent relations with its suppliers.

PRODUKTION (Schriftlich)

Linda Beyer is a management assistant in the store's purchasing department. Her boss is the purchasing manager Steffen Weinhart. Last month, Herr Weinhart ordered some tables from a Swedish company, Hansson Möbler, Stokholmsvägen 1, 151 87 Södertälje, Sweden. The consignment arrived yesterday and unfortunately there are some problems. Herr Weinhart asks Linda to email the Swedish company with a complaint.

YOUR TASK
Use Herr Weinhart's email below to write the email.

Von: steffen.weinhart@lifestyle21.de
An: linda.beyer@lifestyle21.de
Betreff: Beschwerde

Bitte eine E-Mail an Frau Elsa Lundgren bei Hansson Möbler (e.lundgren@hanssonmobler.se) schreiben.

- leider muss ich mich bezüglich unseres Auftrags Nummer 00-A-134 melden
- Waren sind gestern eingegangen
- beim Öffnen des Containers stellten wir fest, dass es zwei Probleme gibt:
  (1) alle Positionen in Kiste Nr. 3 schwer beschädigt
  (2) Kiste 4 enthielt schwarze Tische anstatt der weißen Tische, die wir bestellt hatten
- dies kommt sehr ungelegen, da wir für Ihre Möbel in den letzten zwei Wochen Werbung gemacht haben. Einige unserer besten Kunden haben bereits Interesse bekundet.
- außerdem sind wir für unsere Qualität und den guten Service bekannt
- dem Problem bitte unverzüglich nachgehen
- bitten dringend um Ersatzlieferung
- was sollen wir mit der beschädigten bzw. falschen Ware machen?
- angemessenes Briefende

5 A reminder

SITUATION
Schrift-Art GmbH is a printing company based in Hanover. It specialises in 24-hour and same-day printing for local companies that need brochures, flyers and other sales material quickly. Schrift-Art has a number of regular customers who use their printing services. Once a customer has been with them for some time, it is normal for Schrift-Art to send the customer a monthly bill. The terms of payment are that the account must be settled within 14 days.

PRODUKTION (Schriftlich)
Sie arbeiten in der Verkaufsabteilung bei Schrift-Art. Heute morgen erhalten Sie von Ihrer Chefin Frau Dase diese Notiz.

IHRE AUFGABE
Schreiben Sie den Brief.

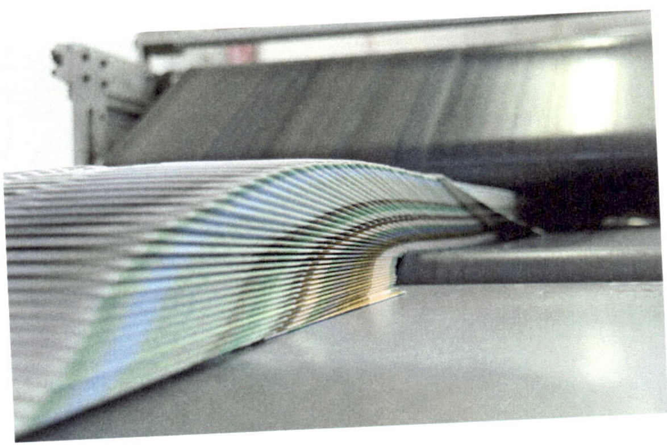

Bitte einen Brief an einen britischen Kunden Herrn Peter Roberts, Bremer Damm 142, 30655 Hannover (Firma: Kostex Ltd.)

- Betreff unsere Rechnung Nr. 817496
- bitte beachten Sie, dass wir noch keine Zahlung für Rechnung Nr ... (s. oben) erhalten haben
- Zahlung sollte innerhalb von 14 Tagen erfolgen
- Kopie der Rechnung liegt bei
- wahrscheinlich ein Versehen aber wir möchten Sie bitten, in den nächsten Tagen Ihre Zahlung anzuweisen
- sollten Sie die Rechnung in der Zwischenzeit beglichen haben, bitten wir Sie diese Mahnung als gegenstandslos zu betrachten
- wir freuen uns auf einen baldigen Ausgleich Ihres Kontos und auf weiterhin gute Zusammenarbeit
- angemessenes Briefende

Practice exam 1

★ Normally, Simone Wilczek, 17, lives in Siegen. But for almost six weeks, she has been in Loimaa, a small town in the south of Finland. Thanks to the European Leonardo da Vinci programme she has the chance to do a 6-week work placement with Rino Lifts Oy, an international company that produces all kinds of truck-mounted lifts*. For the last two weeks, Simone has been in the sales department where she is in contact with customers from all over the world.

* **truck-mounted lifts** *Ladekräne bzw. Hebebühnen, die am LKW montiert sind.*

Teil 1 REZEPTION mündlich (Hörverstehen)

★ Simone's Finnish colleague in the sales department, Aino Soderlund, has taken two days off, so Simone has to answer her phone. When she returns to her desk after lunch, she finds the following message on Aino's answerphone.

YOUR TASK Listen to the message and fill in the information on the message pad.

DATE ______________ 20 ______

MESSAGE FOR ______________________________

TOPIC / CONTRACT / SUBJECT ______________________________

Mr/Ms ______________________________

of ______________________________

in ______________________________ called.

S/he
- ☐ wants you to call back on ______________________
- ☐ will call back again later
- ☐ left the following message:

____

____

____

____

____

____

____

____

____

Teil 2 MEDIATION

★ Juhani Heikkinen, one of Simone's colleagues at Rino Lifts Oy, works in the purchasing department. He sends her the following email asking for a favour:

Hi Simone
I was wondering if you could help us with some German? We are about to start doing business with Lagenfeld AG, a German producer of specialist car bodies from Frankfurt. Of course we are familiar with the products we are considering buying for the production of our new model XT 34D, but I would like some more details about the company itself. Their internet address is www.lagenfeld-karosseriebau.de. I have already found a text which is called "Kurzvorstellung Lagenfeld Karosseriebau". Could you summarise this text in English for me, please?
Regards
Juhani

YOUR TASK Work through the following German text and summarise its main parts in English. Here are some technical terms you need to know:

Karosserie *car body*
Nutzfahrzeug *commercial vehicle*
Schwerlastzugmaschine *heavy-duty haulage truck*
Mehrzweckfahrzeug *multi-purpose vehicle*
Geländefahrzeug *all-terrain vehicle*
Autokran *auto crane*

Lagenfeld Karosseriebau – *darauf können Sie bauen*

Lagenfeld Karosseriebau ist ein mittelständisches Industrieunternehmen in Frankfurt/Main mit 65 Mitarbeitern.

Durch unsere mehr als 40-jährige Erfahrung haben wir uns einen internationalen Namen gemacht, sodass Karosserien made by Lagenfeld mittlerweile auf allen fünf Kontinenten zu finden sind.

Unser Haupttätigkeitsfeld ist die Produktion von speziellen Fahrzeugkarosserien für Nutzfahrzeuge nach den Wünschen unserer Kunden. Als Beispiele können wir hier nennen:

- Schwerlastzugmaschinen
- Mehrzweckfahrzeuge
- Geländefahrzeuge
- Autokrane

Unser Firmensitz ist in Frankfurt. Dort werden in unseren Produktionsanlagen hochwertige Fahrzeugkarosserien gebaut. Unsere Forschungs- und Entwicklungsabteilung arbeitet hier sehr eng mit unseren Kunden zusammen, um deren Wünsche ganz genau umzusetzen. In den ersten Monaten vor Beginn der Produktion besuchen sich Ihre und unsere Spezialisten, um alle Feinheiten zu klären. Auch nachdem unsere Karosserien an Sie ausgeliefert wurden, steht Ihnen unsere Kundenbetreuung weiterhin zur Verfügung.

Also: Was können wir für Sie bauen?

Rufen Sie uns an: 069 / 44 10 43 73-0
oder mailen Sie uns: info@lagenfeld-karosseriebau.de

Teil 3 REZEPTION Leseverstehen

★ Rino Lifts Oy is considering including truck-mounted forklifts in their range of products. Simone finds the following text which gives her a better idea of this product.

YOUR TASK Read the text about truck-mounted forklifts *(Gabelstapler)* and write notes to complete the table in English.

Truck-mounted forklifts (TMFs)

Truck-mounted forklifts (TMFs) make the transport of any kind of goods fast and convenient. These mobile forklifts are mounted on the rear of a truck and can be dismounted in less than a minute. The clear advantage of a TMF is that truck drivers do not have to wait for help to unload their truck. That saves a lot of time and labour costs. Truck-mounted forklifts can lift up to 3.5 tonnes.

The world's biggest TMF producers are to be found in Ireland and in the USA. Both are a part of Hiab Oy, a company owned by Cargotec Corp of Helsinki, Finland.

Experts estimate that the annual market size of truck-mounted cargo lifts is at least 6,000 units. Approximately 50% of the units are sold in North America; about 2,000 TMFs are bought by European companies. At the moment, the TMF market is said to grow 5 to 10% per annum. When talking to TMF manufacturers, however, it is extremely hard to get more detailed sales figures. But all producers in this field of business say that the industry is intensely competitive.

In the USA and Canada, the world's biggest TMF market, the building materials industry is the TMF industry's most important customer constituting more than 70% of the forklift sales. 15% are from agriculture and the rest from other industries and businesses.

Aspect	Information from the text
TMFs in general (product description)	
TMF producers	
TMF markets	

Teil 4 PRODUKTION schriftlich

(Verfassen eines englischsprachigen Briefes nach Stichworten)

Rino Lifts Oy is moving towards a paperless office!

★ The headline above states the management's goals for next year. Because of this the company's purchasing manager asks Simone to write enquiries for:

1. fast document management scanners,
2. document management software.

Simone does some research on the internet and comes up with the address of VisionScan Ltd, 35 Belgrave Road, Nottingham NG5 9RA UK.

Here are her notes:

- Adresse im Internet gefunden
- wir sind mittelständischer Hersteller von Kranwagen in Finnland
- sind auf dem Weg zum papierlosen Büro: benötigen 75 Dokumentenscanner und Software
- sollen schnell, verlässlich und einfach zu handhaben sein
- Installation muss leicht sein
- benötigen ein Seminar zur Einführung
- bitte Informationsmaterialien und Preisliste schicken
- erwarten wettbewerbsfähigen Preis
- Angemessenes Briefende

YOUR TASK Write Simone's enquiry for document scanners and document management software based on her notes.

Teil 5 PRODUKTION eigene Stellungnahme

★ Rino Lifts Oy's management has decided that the company should substantially increase its green image. Therefore they have taken the following decisions:

1. Rino Lift Oy will install an independent block power station running on solar and wind energy. This way, they will produce 50% of their own energy.
2. By 2012, Rino Lift Oy will transport 65% of their products by rail and ship.
3. Rino Lift Oy will produce an auto crane which runs on biodiesel.

However, recent calculations have shown that these measures will increase the prices of all Rino Lifts products by a minimum of 7%.

YOUR TASK Comment on the pros and cons of Rino Lifts management decisions. Give reasons for your opinion.

Practice exam 2

★ Toysworld GmbH is a German wholesaler of entertainment and education goods for children. Karsten Ditschke is a management assistant in the purchasing department.

Teil 1 REZEPTION mündlich (Hörverstehen)

★ As Toysworld GmbH is always looking for new trends on the global market, Karsten Ditschke often has to listen to English radio stations. This is part of a programme about Playlearn Ltd., a producer of kids' toys in Hong Kong.

YOUR TASK **Listen to the programme and complete the following table in English.**

Aspect	Information
the company	
its customers	
product range	
product development	
the new Kids' Computer	

Teil 2 REZEPTION Leseverstehen

★ Toysworld GmbH watches the global market for new trends in entertainment and education, but also follows current marketing strategies. Karsten Ditschke finds the following article about marketing to kids in an American trade journal.

YOUR TASK Read the article and write notes to complete the table in English.

Many scientists and educators openly criticise the increased trend of marketing to kids and teenagers. Looking at the billions of dollars spent on advertising worldwide every year, they question why more and more of this is aimed at young children. For advertisers this trend is very logical. Firstly, there is the huge amount of money which children spend themselves; secondly, children have a considerable influence on their parents' spending; and finally the same children will one day spend money as adults.

Critics, however, raise serious questions about the ability of children to understand what advertising is. According to numerous studies, children are unlikely to grasp the intention of advertisers.

In the past marketing to kids used to concentrate mainly on sweets and toys, but now it also includes computer and entertainment products, clothes and shoes, fast food, sports equipment etc. Nowdays, even advertising for products such as cars, holidays or credit cards is aimed at children.

Researchers state that older children are more able to differentiate between reality and advertising, but even they can be easily influenced by advertisers. Since children are only beginning to form their own identities, they tend to conform to group standards. They often feel insecure and want to belong to their peer group. Consequently, marketing and advertising campaigns encourage them to find happiness and self esteem through consumption.

For the advertising industry, children and teenagers represent a very important market. In the US, school-age children and teenagers spend more than $100 billion of their own and their family's money each year. Additionally, they influence family spending decisions when it comes to buying food, household items, electrical appliances and computers, holiday trips, the family car etc. Children are also the key to future sales. Advertisers and scientists have found out that that brand loyalties and consumer habits which are formed when young will be carried through to adulthood.

Aspect	Information
Marketing facts, new developments	
Main points of criticism	
Reasons why children are targeted	

Teil 3 MEDIATION

★ Karsten's boss is about to attend an international toy fair. In order to prepare for his meetings there, he asks Karsten for a short English summary of the following text.

YOUR TASK **Summarize the most important aspects of the following text in English.**

Die letzten Wochen des Jahres sind für den Spielwarenmarkt in Deutschland von immenser Bedeutung, denn die Branche macht hier über 40 Prozent ihres Gesamtumsatzes. Das bedeutet auch, dass diese eine Zeit von sehr hartem Wettbewerb ist, auf den sich Groß- und Einzelhändler vorbereiten müssen. Deshalb benötigt jedes Unternehmen ein umfassendes Maßnahmenpaket, das sich unter anderem aus den folgenden Bestandteilen zusammensetzt:

- eine attraktive und zeitgemäße Produktauswahl, die die Kunden anzieht,
- eine ausgeklügelte Marketingstrategie, die auf die Zielgruppen abgestimmt ist,
- flexible Rabatte, um auf die jeweilige Lage vor Ort zu reagieren.

Die großen national operierenden Spielwarenketten starten jährlich in Zusammenarbeit mit den wichtigsten Spielwarenherstellern Werbekampagnen im Massenmedium Fernsehen. Spezielle TV-Spots werden produziert, die die Weihnachtshighlights für die Kinder und Jugendlichen präsentieren. Darüber hinaus gibt es eine große Vielfalt an Gesamt- und speziellen Themenkatalogen, die im Einzelhandel ausliegen oder auch per Post an die Haushalte geschickt werden. Schließlich gibt es unterschiedliche Gewinnspiele mit attraktiven Preisen, bei denen man die Lösungen per Post, im Internet oder im Geschäft selbst abgeben kann.

Teil 4 PRODUKTION schriftlich

(Verfassen eines englischsprachigen Briefes nach Stichworten)

★ After Karsten Ditschke told his boss about the new Kids' Computer Playlearn Limited produces, he is asked to contact the company in Hong Kong. Here are the German notes Karsten should use:

Bitte Anfrage nach neuen Kindercomputern an Playlearn Ltd in Hong Kong schreiben (Adresse: 21/F, One Kowloon, 1 Wang Yuen Street, Kowloon Bay, Hong Kong).

- Vorstellung unseres Unternehmens: expandierender Großhandel für Kinderspielzeug, Schwerpunkt Deutschland und deutschsprachiges Ausland
- im Radio über diesen Computer gehört
- Bitte um Zusendung von Verkaufsbroschüren und Preislisten
- Bitte um zwei Computern zu Testzwecken
- da Spielwarenmarkt ein sehr umkämpfter Markt ist, kommen nur qualitativ hochwertige und wettbewerbsfähige Produkte in Betracht
- wenn Kindercomputer überzeugen kann, sind regelmäßige Folgeaufträge wahrscheinlich
- einzige Bedingung für Geschäftsbeziehung: Toysworld GmbH muss Alleinimporteur für den Kindercomputer in Deutschland sein

Teil 5 PRODUKTION eigene Stellungnahme

Toyworld has negotiated a contract to sell Playlearn's computer in Germany. They are now thinking of a suitable advertising campaign. Should this be aimed directly at children? Discuss the pros and cons. Give reasons for your opinion.

Practice exam 3

★ Heek & Treckendorf is a fashion chain store operating all over Germany. Margit Lütkebohmert works as an assistant to the purchasing manager, Rilke Tomberg. As Rilke Tomberg is responsible for buying the fashion H & T sells in its stores, she and her team are always on the lookout for new trends. Recently she discovered a new young fashion label called BBB WorldWear.

Teil 1 REZEPTION mündlich (Hörverstehen)

★ Margit Lütkebohmert listens to a radio interview with BBB WorldWear which was given after this year's trade fair in New York.

YOUR TASK **Add notes to the headings in the diagram with information from the listening text.**

Origins

What does 'global' mean for BBB Worldwear?

Production

Fashion / styles

Teil 2 REZEPTION Leseverstehen

★ The international fashion magazine WEAREVER found out about an emerging partnership between BBB WorldWear and Heek & Treckendorf. They asked for an interview with the purchasing manager, Rilke Tomberg. So Margit Lütkebohmert has to prepare some statements for the interview and reads the following text about the global fashion industry.

YOUR TASK **Work through the text and complete the following table.**

The textile industry with all its suppliers is one of the most globalized industries. In almost every country in the world, various types of clothes are produced from a huge range of textiles. Often these goods will later on be sold somewhere else.

The clothing industry makes up the largest source of industrial employment in the world. That means that about 30 million people are making clothes and textiles across the globe. Increasingly, clothing imported to the Western world comes from developing countries such as Honduras and Bangladesh, as many multinational clothing manufacturers have decided to move their production facilities to places with lower working standards. China, Bangladesh, and Honduras are among the most popular. China, for example, has in the meantime emerged as the largest exporter of what is sometimes called fast fashion, accounting for 30% of world fashion exports.

Many emerging economies are aiming to get their share of the world's fashion markets even if the fierce global competition demands ever lower production costs. Very often, however, this results in lower wages and poor conditions for workers. However, in many Asian countries, despite these working conditions, the clothing industry is one of the most important employers. Due to the scarcity of employment in these countries, globalization in the textile industry provides a welcome number of jobs.

The fast fashion industry leaves a large pollution footprint with each step of the clothing life cycle. For example, polyester, the most widely used manufactured fibre, is made from petroleum. The demand for this energy-intensive material has nearly doubled in the last 15 years. Cotton, one of the most popular and versatile fibres used in clothing manufacture, also has a significant environmental footprint. It accounts for a quarter of all the pesticides used in the United States, the largest exporter of cotton in the world.

Aspect	Information
Production	
Employment	
Ecology	

Teil 3 MEDIATION

★ While preparing for the interview, WEAREVER, the fashion magazine, asks for Heek & Treckendorf's position on globalization and the fashion industry. So Rilke Tomberg asks her assistant Margit Lütkebohmert to summarize the following statement in English.

YOUR TASK Summarize the following statement in English.

Als börsennotierte Familienunternehmen mit Gewinnorientierung sind wir bei Heek & Treckendorf Teil der großen globalen Beschaffungsnetze der Welt. Wie alle international agierenden Handelskonzerne muss auch Heek & Treckendorf weltweit die günstigsten Einkaufsquellen für seine Produkte suchen, um unseren Kunden wettbewerbsfähige Preise anbieten zu können.

Durch die Suche nach neuen Herstellern bzw. Lieferanten besonders im asiatischen Raum verbessert sich Heek & Treckendorfs Marge um zehn bis 15 Prozent. Das Geld, was hier eingespart wird, sichert auf lange Sicht Arbeitsplätze in Deutschland.

Trotz der intensiven Suche nach sehr wettbewerbsfähigen Konditionen auf einem globalisierten Markt sind für Heek & Treckendorf faire Arbeitsbedingungen und Bezahlung wichtig. Wir möchten die Chancen, die die Globalisierung für unsere Kunden in Form von großer Produktvielfalt und konkurrenzfähigen Preisen bringt, auch in den Herkunftsländern umgesetzt sehen. Globalisierung bringt hier dringend benötigte Arbeitsplätze. Hier ist es ein Teil von Heek & Treckendorfs Verantwortung in einer globalisierten Welt, dafür zu sorgen, dass diese Arbeitsplätze fair ausgestaltet und auf lange Sicht erhalten bleiben.

globale Beschaffungsnetze *global supply networks*

Teil 4 PRODUKTION schriftlich

(Verfassen eines englischsprachigen Briefes nach Stichworten)

★ As Heek & Treckendorf are very interested in including BBB WORLDWEAR's fashion in their range of products, Rilke Tomberg gets in touch with the young fashion label company again. On the phone they agree to meet so that BBB WORLDWEAR can present their collection to Heek & Treckendorf. Margit Lütkebohmert has to send a summary of the phone conversation to BBB WORLDWEAR.

YOUR TASK Write a letter to be signed by Rilke Tomberg using the following notes:

An Piet Smets, BBB WORLDWEAR, 1 Chapel Court, London, SE1 1HH, Great Britain
Bezug auf Telefonat vom 22.11.

- anbei schriftliche Zusammenfassung der Ergebnisse
- Danke für Gelegenheit, das Fashion Label kennen zu lernen
- erster Eindruck: halten BBB WORLDWEARs Mode für aktuell, modern und vielfältig
- Terminbestätigung: 10.12. 10 – 18 Uhr im Regent's Hotel, London
- Bitte um Vorführung der aktuellen Kollektion
- in der Zwischenzeit: bitte um Zusendung aktueller Katalog und Preislisten
- Verweis auf unsere Internetseite www.heek-treckendorf.de

Teil 5 PRODUKTION eigene Stellungnahme

Using your background knowledge of the globalized fashion industry, comment on the fact that the majority of the clothes we buy in Germany are produced in developing countries. Include the arguments for and against this situation.

Bildquellennachweis

Cover Fuchs, Kurt, Erlangen; **Cover** Corbis (George Hammerstein/Solus-Veer), Düsseldorf; **8** iStockphoto (blue_iq), Calgary, Alberta; **9** JupiterImages photos.com, Tucson, AZ; **9** iStockphoto (Jacob Wackerhausen), Calgary, Alberta; **10** iStockphoto (Rich Legg), Calgary, Alberta; **10** shutterstock (CURAphotography), New York, NY; **12** shutterstock (Zsolt Nyulaszi), New York, NY; **14** JupiterImages photos.com, Tucson, AZ; **16** Klett-Archiv (A. Raftaki), Stuttgart; **17** shutterstock (Debra James), New York, NY; **18** shutterstock (Cynthia Farmer), New York, NY; **19** shutterstock (Konstantin Chagin), New York, NY; **20** iStockphoto (Jacom Stephens), Calgary, Alberta; **21** Jupiterimages GmbH (clipart.com), Ottobrunn/München; **24** Jupiterimages GmbH (clipart.com), Ottobrunn/München; **24** iStockphoto (fatcat21), Calgary, Alberta; **25** shutterstock (kristian sekulic), New York, NY; **26** JupiterImages photos.com, Tucson, AZ; **27** JupiterImages photos.com, Tucson, AZ; **29** shutterstock (Peter Elvidge), New York, NY; **29** MEV Verlag GmbH, Augsburg; **31** shutterstock (Lelde J-R), New York, NY; **31** shutterstock (Paul Bodea), New York, NY; **31** shutterstock (Raphael Daniaud), New York, NY; **35** shutterstock (Lasse Kristensen), New York, NY; **35** shutterstock (Monkey Business Images), New York, NY; **37** JupiterImages photos.com, Tucson, AZ; **39** shutterstock (Yuri Arcurs), New York, NY; **39** shutterstock (Galyna Andrushko), New York, NY; **39** shutterstock (Adisa), New York, NY; **39** shutterstock (Naturaldigital), New York, NY; **40** BBC Information and archives, London; **41** shutterstock (Liv friis-larsen), New York, NY; **42** shutterstock (Sapsiwai), New York, NY; **43** shutterstock (Péter Gudella), New York, NY; **45** JupiterImages photos.com, Tucson, AZ; **47** shutterstock (Mark Winfrey), New York, NY; **48** shutterstock (Darren Baker), New York, NY; **48** shutterstock (1971yes), New York, NY; **48** iStockphoto (Otmar Smit), Calgary, Alberta; **48** iStockphoto (Lena Andersson), Calgary, Alberta; **49** shutterstock (Anyka), New York, NY; **51** AKG, Berlin; **52** BBC Information and archives, London; **53** shutterstock (Miroslav Tolimir), New York, NY; **58** shutterstock (Yuri Arcurs), New York, NY; **58** shutterstock (Igor Stepovik), New York, NY; **58** shutterstock (Andre Blais), New York, NY; **59** shutterstock (Konstantin Sutyagin), New York, NY; **60** shutterstock (Dmitriy Shironosov), New York, NY; **61** shutterstock (Steve Luker), New York, NY; **63** shutterstock (Mark Yuill), New York, NY; **67** iStockphoto (Joao Virissimo), Calgary, Alberta; **68** iStockphoto (Mark McDonald), Calgary, Alberta; **68** iStockphoto (Phillip Jones), Calgary, Alberta; **73** shutterstock (Supri Suharjoto), New York, NY; **73** iStockphoto (Diana Starobinskaya), Calgary, Alberta; **74** shutterstock (Magdalena Bujak), New York, NY; **77** iStockphoto (Ed Hidden), Calgary, Alberta; **77** JupiterImages photos.com, Tucson, AZ; **78** shutterstock (Oceania), New York, NY; **79** shutterstock (AMA), New York, NY; **80** BBC Information and archives, London; **82** iStockphoto (murat en), Calgary, Alberta; **83** iStockphoto (Jillian Pond), Calgary, Alberta; **83** iStockphoto (Atlee Mercer), Calgary, Alberta; **84** iStockphoto (fotoIE), Calgary, Alberta; **84** JupiterImages photos.com, Tucson, AZ; **84** shutterstock (dainis), New York, NY; **85** shutterstock (Michele Perbellini), New York, NY

Nicht in allen Fällen war es uns möglich, den Rechteinhaber der Abbildungen ausfindig zu machen. Berechtigte Ansprüche werden selbstverständlich im Rahmen der üblichen Vereinbarungen abgegolten.

D

1 b; 2 a; 3 b; 4 a; 5 b; 6 c; 7 a; 8 c; 9 b; 10 a

TIPPS zu D Grundwortschatz

Am Anfang eines jeden Ausbildungsgangs wird von den Lernern erwartet, dass sie einen 'Grundwortschatz' beherrschen. Die gerade gelöste Aufgabe hat stichpunktartig diesen überprüft.

Sollten Sie einige Worte nicht gewusst haben, beginnen Sie bitte mit der Wiederholung des Grundwortschatzes, den Sie als Vokabellernliste auf Ihrer DVD im Schülerbuch finden. Am besten Sie gehen diesen gleich einmal durch. Das erleichtert Ihnen enorm die weitere Arbeit.

E

1. I think (that) the world of work is very interesting.
2. Lots of (A lot of) my friends work in offices.
3. After my exam, I'd like to work in an office, too. (I'd also like to work in an office.)
4. It is easy nowadays to work abroad.
5. I like travelling and perhaps (maybe) one day I'll work in the USA or (in) Great Britain.
6. English is sometimes difficult (hard)! It is very important, however, to learn the language. English is a world language.

TIPPS zu E Schreiben (Sprachmittlung)

Das Schreiben ist für manche wohl die schwierigste aller Kompetenzen, ob man frei schreibt oder wie hier Sätze übersetzt. Im Laufe der Arbeit mit *Business Expert* werden Sie immer wieder aufgefordert, diese Kompetenz zu trainieren und erhalten verschiedene Hilfestellungen, mit denen Sie Ihr Schreiben verbessern.

Sollten Sie hier einige Sätze nicht korrekt wiedergegeben haben, konzentrieren Sie sich besonders auf die E-Teile, *Be an English expert!* sowie die *Phrases* (Redemittel), die – in den *Units* sowie zusammengefasst ebenfalls auf der DVD – neben vielen anderen Aufgaben besonders Ihre Schreibfähigkeit verbessern helfen.

Unit 1

A

1

1. *Ireland*
2. UK
3. Denmark
4. (the) Netherlands
5. Sweden
6. Finland
7. Estonia
8. Latvia
9. Lithuania
10. Poland
11. Germany
12. Belgium
13. Luxembourg
14. France
15. Portugal
16. Spain
17. Italy
18. Austria
19. Czech Republic
20. Slovakia
21. Hungary
22. Slovenia
23. Romania
24. Bulgaria
25. Cyprus
26. Greece
27. Malta

1 27
2 Turkey
3 Norway
4 Switzerland
5 (19)93
6 1951
7 travel
8 work
9 nationalities
10 euro
11 Eurozone
12 Britain / the UK

B

1

C eine zeitlich begrenzte Handlung in der Gegenwart
A Handlungen in der Gegenwart, die auf Dauer gültig sind
D Zukunftspläne
B Ereignisse in der Vergangenheit

2

1 *come*
2 live
3 wasn't born
4 lived
5 moved
6 was
7 went
8 left
9 'm studying
10 'm enjoying
11 want
12 'm going to work
13 visited
14 loved
15 plan
16 'd like / would like

3

1 *is*
2 is
3 works
4 likes
5 has
6 thinks
7 isn't
8 's doing
9 's spending
10 's training
11 is
12 'm learning
13 like
14 want

4

1 *do you come*
2 are you spending here?
3 What course are you doing? (...are you on?)
4 did you come here?
5 do you like the town?

5

Individuelle Lösungen

D

1

1 *o*; 2 h; 3 i; 4 j; 5 b; 6 a; 7 g; 8 d; 9 c; 10 n; 11 m; 12 k; 13 f; 14 e; 15 l

1. *law*
2. in favour of
3. currency
4. parliament
5. standard of living
6. War
7. alternative
8. unthinkable
9. mobile
10. democracy, right

2

a trading bloc
b consumer
c environment
d education system

Beispiellösungen
a With 500 million people, the EU is the world's biggest trading bloc.
b Food labelling helps consumers to know what is in a food product.
c We all want a clean and green environment.
d The education system in Germany is different from the education system in the UK.

3 EXTRA

1. *Finn, Finnish*
2. Pole, Polish
3. Portuguese
4. Belgians
5. Norwegians
6. Irishwoman
7. Bulgarian, Italian, Hungarian
8. Swiss
9. Spaniard
10. Icelandic
11. Turkish

Video lounge

1

1. *supposed*, my mind
2. baggage allowance
3. hang out with
4. easy reach
5. enrol
6. start … scratch
7. together
8. pretty much
9. transition, readjusting
10. working on
11. something … going on

2

Beispiellösungen
Section 1
1. Paris. She visited a friend in Berlin in November and came back for New Year. She (just) had a good feeling about Berlin.
2. Thousands of lakes and forests and places like Wannsee. Everyone decamps to the beach.
3. Three or four friends (from London). Extra baggage allowance.
4. She had no home, no job, and couldn't speak the language.
5. She got her bike, enrolled at a language school, found a place to live and is now working on finding a job.

Section 2
6. She started with some language books. She found the books in a box in the street in a part of London called Soho.
7. She's learning German. She has friends there and it gives her a social life.

Section 3
8. They were shocked and surprised that Seema didn't go to Paris (as expected). Later, they were 'cool'.
9. It's easy to move around. There are people from around the world in every city. There's a real European culture thing going on. Seema thinks young people should 'go out there, try it.'

3

Beispiellösung
Seema Prabhu is a 26-year-old English journalist who is living in Berlin at the moment. She came to Berlin after a couple of visits to the city because she liked it so much. Seema's life in Berlin was hard at first. She didn't speak German, and she didn't have a flat or a job. Now she is happy there. One important thing for her was enrolling at a language school. She learned German there and she also met lots of people. Seema's parents were surprised when she went to Berlin (she was supposed to go to Paris). But now they are 'cool' about it. Seema thinks that all young people should travel. She believes there's a 'European culture thing going on'.
(121 words)

Unit 2

1

Land / Stadt	*(Republik) Irland / Shannon*
Art des Unternehmens	Flughafen
Art der Tätigkeit(en)	Arbeit in den Marketing und Luftfrachtabteilungen des Flughafens
Voraussetzungen	Bewerber müssen zwischen 18 und 25 Jahre alt sein / über ausgezeichnete Computer- und gute Englischkentinisse verfügen
Bezahlung	Monatlicher Lohn von €450
Unterkunft	Entweder bei irischen Familien im Ort oder in einem internationalen Studentenheim 1 km vom Flughafen entfernt
Name der Kontaktperson	Linda Kearney

2

1 Walkenweg 17
33605 Bielefeld
Germany
2 Ms Linda Kearney
Shannon Airport
County Clare
Ireland
3 Dear Ms Kearney
4 Application for an internship at Shannon Airport
5 IrelandLink
6 two-year full-time Business and Administration course
7 Bielefeld
8 a 'Speditionskaufmann' (management assistant in freight forwarding)
9 a four-week work placement in the freight forwarding department of a large German logistics company
10 football, hockey and ice skating
11 Yours sincerely
12 Encl.: CV

3

1. *Dear Mr MacKenzie*
2. I would like to apply for the work placement which you advertised on the Canada Tourism website.
3. I am currently in the second year of a two-year course at a

vocational college in Cologne, Germany.
4. As you will see from my CV, I have good English and computer skills.
5. I am hard working, keen to learn, and a good communicator.
6. I have previous work experience in the hotel industry. Last year in my summer holidays I worked in an international hotel in Turkey.
7. My interests include sport, music and dance (dancing).
8. I would very much welcome the opportunity to work in a Canadian hotel.
9. I hope that you will consider my application and I look forward to hearing from you.
10. Yours sincerely

4

Land / Stadt	Australien / Sydney
Art des Unternehmens	Rundfunkgesellschaft
Art der Tätigkeit(en)	Arbeit bei ABC Commercial: internationale Verkaufs- und Marketingabteilung
Voraussetzungen	Bewerber müssen zwischen 18 und 30 Jahre alt sein / über gute Englisch- sowie Internet- und Computerkenntnisse verfügen / gut in einem Team arbeiten können / kommunikative Menschen sein / energisch und enthusiastisch sein
Bezahlung	AU$800 (monatlich)
Unterkunft	Studentenheim im Ort (umsonst)
Name der Kontaktperson	Julie Cameron (E-Mail: julie.cameron@abc_commercial.au)

Beispiellösung

Dear Ms Cameron

I would like to apply for one of the work placements which you advertised on the Praktikumsbörse.de website. I would be interested in a six month placement. I would be available to start work (take up the placement) in July.

I am currently in the second year of a two-year full-time course in business administration at a vocational college in Dortmund, Germany. After finishing my course, I will obtain my qualification as a management assistant (Kauffrau). This is equivalent to a BTEC National Certificate in Australia. I therefore have a good basic knowledge of marketing and of office administration.

As you will see from my enclosed CV, I have a good knowledge of English and good (advanced) internet and computer skills. My college teachers tell me that I work well in a team, am a good communicator, and have plenty of energy and enthusiasm. I have a wide range of interests including all sports, fitness and travel.

I would very much welcome the opportunity to work at ABC Commercial. I hope that you will consider my application and look forward to hearing from you soon.

Yours sincerely

5 ROUNDUP

1. *to apply*, application
2. applicant
3. internship
4. advertisement
5. advertised
6. currently
7. hard working, keen to learn, reliable, a good communicator
8. A good knowledge of English
9. unpaid, wage

Unit 3

A

1

1. *main entrance*
2. restaurant
3. customer service
4. archive
5. reception
6. meeting rooms
7. accounts
8. production, purchasing, logistics
9. marketing, sales
10. IT, HR

2

1. *is responsible for selling Falke's products.*
2. is responsible for looking after the company's money.
3. is responsible for buying raw materials.
4. is responsible for looking after the computer network.
5. is responsible for distributing the company's products.
6. is responsible for dealing with customers' problems.

B

1

1 *which*
2 who
3 which / that
4 which / that
5 who

2

1a *S*
1b O
2a S
2b O
3a O
3b S
4a O
4b S

Wenn *who, which* und *that* Subjekt sind, folgt direkt ein Verb ('a firm which makes'). Wenn sie Objekt sind, folgt auf das Relativpronomen ein Substantiv oder Personalpronomen ('the job which Ivan has')

3

1. The building (...) you can see on page 18 is the headquarters of Falke GmbH.
2. He enjoys speaking English with the people (...) he meets.
3. He likes seeing the places (...) he visits.
4. The city (...) he liked best was Seattle.

4

Beispiellösung: Welcome again to Falke, Mr Corff. I'd like to tell you first a little bit about our company. We're the largest manufacturer of bicycle tyres in Germany. We operate worldwide and have sales offices in 24 countries. We're based in Germany. Our headquarters are here in Remagen. (All our major departments are here except one): our R&D department is in Bonn. (We don't manufacture our products in Germany). We have production facilities in Korea and Lithuania. Falke was founded in 1923. The founders were two brothers, Willi and Albrecht Kaiser. The firm is still family owned and the present owner is the great-granddaughter of Albrecht Kaiser / Albrecht Kaiser's great-granddaughter.

D

1

Business (What kind of company? Product(s)?)
manufacturer, cycles, cycling accessories, flagship product: Mountain Ace 800

Interesting fact?
started in a barn on a farm

Founded (When? By?)
1976, Steve Beglinger and Elizabeth Proznik

Turnover (How much does it earn?)
last year $607 million

Headquarters (Where is it based?)
Janesville Wisconsin (USA)

Employees (How many people work for the company?)
1,500 (850 in factory in Janesville)

Operations (Where does it sell its products? How? And in the future?)
all 50 American states and since 2008 in Canada, only through specialist dealers, planning to start selling in Europe

2 Individuelle Lösung

3 EXTRA

1. *fifth*
2. nineteen twenty-three, nineteen seventy-six
3. two thousand and two
4. twenty twelve
5. two thirds
6. (a) half
7. one point two billion euros
8. two point seven six million euros
9. nineteen oh three / nineteen hundred and three
10. eighteen eighty-three

Video lounge

1

1. *compare*
2. bring
3. gimmick
4. see through
5. great believer
6. the basis that
7. key thing
8. immersed
9. over her shoulder
10. reckon

2

Beispiellösungen
Section 1
almost certainly do what you shouldn't do.

Section 2
He decided they looked boring, didn't work very well, and were designed by people with no enthusiasm. Windsurfers, surfboards, skis, skates were made by enthusiasts. They loved their products but vacuum cleaner manufacturers didn't love their products.

Section 3
He says he's a great believer in focusing and concentrating. He was happy about the situation because he is always happy just doing one thing.

Section 4
(a) People see through gimmicks very quickly and his vacuum cleaners wouldn't sell if they were just gimmicks. (b) He didn't advertise the product. It was successful because it worked well and people told other people about it. (Note: This is often called *word of mouth advertising* – 'Mundpropaganda').

Section 5
False. The really important things for Mr Dyson are: people love his product; he likes making something 'with your own hands'.

Section 6
False. You shouldn't worry because 50% of your decision will always be wrong.

Section 7
The key thing for him is the product. People don't buy his vacuum cleaners because they're interested in his company. They want a good product.

3

Beispiellösung: It is difficult to talk about a 'typical' businessman. I think all businesspeople are different. However, Mr Dyson has some ideas that are very interesting and he is perhaps different from many other businesspeople. I think one important thing is that he is very enthusiastic about his products. He also wants to make very good products and he isn't interested in 'gimmicks'. He is also not afraid to make mistakes. I think that's good. Perhaps his most interesting idea is that he isn't a businessman because he wants to be rich. The key things are to enjoy his work and to sell good vacuum cleaners. (105 words)

Unit 4

1

1. *mike.harris@google.com*
2. l.williams@bt-online.co.uk
3. ina.krueger@web.de
4. liv.wagner@nordfracht_sales.de
5. bodo-richter@koeln_net.de

2

1. *Would you please send me the dates of the trade fair next month?*
2. Would / Could you please email me the name of your new sales manager?

3. Would / Could you please let me have the name of your logistics company?
4. *Could you tell me / let me know when you will send your report?*
5. Could you tell me / let me know where your sales offices in the Netherlands are?
6. Could you tell me / let me know if you have Ms Jones's mobile number?
7. Would / Could you please email me the dates when your office will be closed?
8. Could you tell me / let me know if someone will meet me at the airport?
9. Could you tell me / let me know where your new factory is?
10. Would / Could you please let us have your decision asap?

3

1. Melissa Taylor (24 October 17.15) wants some sales literature. Melissa again (24 October 17.25) wants the dates of Ms Dabbert's next visit to the UK.
2. Rafael Costa is sending you details of the trade fair in Rio de Janeiro. Wim de Vries is letting you know the Amsterdam office will be closed on 28 and 29 November.

4

Rafael
1 the trade fair in Rio de Janeiro next month.
2 Could you please send
3 in advance

Beispiellösungen

Melissa (E-Mail 1)
Dear Melissa
Thanks for your email. We're also excited about the product launch. Sales brochures will be available on 15 November. We'll send them to you immediately by post.
Best regards

Melissa (E-Mail 2)
Hello again Melissa
I'm attaching the details of Ms Dabbert's next trip. We can book hotels here, but would you please organise / arrange for a hire car? Thanks!
With best wishes

Wim
Thank you for the information.
Please let us you if you will be contactable / if we will be able to contact you by phone on the 28th and 29th. Do you have a mobile number for us?
Would you also please send us your monthly sales figures for November by 27 November?
Good luck with the move / reorganisation.
All the best

5 ROUNDUP

1. *in*	8. sorry
2. attachment	9. afraid
3. let	10. open
4. forward	11. things
5. wanted	12. Fine
6. asked	13. attaching
7. further	14. Could / Would

Unit 5

A

1 1 *a*; 2 e; 3 i; 4 j; 5 h; 6 b; 7 c; 8 d; 9 f; 10 g

1. *looks after*	5. books, reserves
2. sits in on, takes	6. listens to
3. writes up	7. has
4. makes	

2

1 Certainly.
2 Could I speak to
3 Who's calling
4 This is
5 Would you spell your name for me, please?
6 One moment, please. I'm putting you through now.

B

1 1 *d*; 2 e; 3 a; 4 f; 5 c; 6 b; 7 b

2 *On*, at; On, at; In, in

Beispiellösungen
1. *On Monday morning at* 9.30 he's having a meeting with the marketing team. In the afternoon he's interviewing applicants for an IT technician's job. On Tuesday morning he's having brunch with Steffen and Jakob from image22 and in the afternoon he's having a meeting with Katja Wingartz.
2. On Wednesday morning he's preparing a presentation for Saturday and on Wednesday afternoon he's visiting RAZ's printing works.
3. He isn't coming into the office on Thursday. He's working at home all day.
4. At 9.00 on Friday morning he's having a meeting with the sales manager. At 15.14 on Friday afternoon he's travelling to Amsterdam.
5. On Saturday morning he's attending a conference in Amsterdam and at 2.45 pm on Saturday afternoon he's making a presentation at the conference. He's returning to Dusseldorf at 5.34 pm.

3

1. *It* begins at 8.00 pm on Friday.
2. It ends at 4.00 pm on Saturday.
3. It leaves at 15.14.
4. It takes two hours (and) eleven minutes.
5. He leaves Amsterdam at 17.34 and he arrives back in Dusseldorf at 19.46.

4

1 Mr Holweg's itinerary 18–19 May

by train to Amsterdam and will be arriving on 18 May at 17.25. He will be staying overnight at the Amsterdam Hilton (Tel: +31-20-710 60 00, Fax: +31-20-710 60 80). He will be returning to Dusseldorf on 19 May at 17.34. Please let me know if you have any further questions / need any further information.
Yours sincerely

D

1

Down		Across	
1	facilities	5	guest
2	friendly	7	air conditioned
3	book	8	secretarial
4	receptionist	10	continental
6	equipped	11	per
9	stars	14	service
12	include	16	hairdryer
13	airport	17	located
15	en suite	18	alarm
17	laundry	19	single
18	access	21	luxury
20	gym	23	double
22	walk	27	maker
24	bar	28	sauna
25	quiet		
26	fax		

2

1. *oh one two eight six*, double two five, eight double four
2. oh two oh, four five three nine, eight double oh
3. four one seven, two nine nine, zero eight zero eight
4. two one two, two zero one, nine nine six two

1 *I'm afraid he's in a meeting right now.*
2 Can he call you back in about half an hour?
3 This is
4 Does Kris have your phone number, Ms Bell?
5 I'll give it to you again.
6 I'll just repeat that.
7 I'll tell Kris as soon as he comes out of the meeting.
8 You're welcome

E

1

1. *availability?*
2. solve
3. translate
4. comfortable
5. flight
6. located
7. arrangements
8. fitness
9. expense

Beispiellösungen: We had a long discussion about the problem. / Our discussion lasted three hours.

Unit 6

1

Unternehmen	Hersteller von Schallisolierungsmaterialien – #1 in Norwegen – vor über 40 Jahren gegründet (– führende Stelle auf dem skandinavischen Markt)
Produkte / Anwendungen	umfassendes Sortiment von Produkten – 10–20% wirksamer als Produkte von Hauptkonkurrenten – Isolierung für Wände, Decken, Fußböden – Anwendung in Privathäusern und öffentlichen Gebäuden (z. B. Schulen, Büros, Freizeitzentren, Kinos)
Weitere Dienstleistungen	Beratung und technische Unterstützung vom Expertenteam
Kontakt	Adresse: Ro AS, N-6146 Aheim, Norway – Email: info@ro.com – Internet: www.ro.com

2

(3) Why you are writing and what you would like
1. *e;* 2. a, 3. c

(1) Where you found out about a supplier
4. d, 5. g

(4) Ending your letter
6. f

(2) Your company
7. b; 8. h; 9. i

3

1. *You were recommended to us*
2. leading German company.
3. If your prices are competitive
4. possible discounts
5. samples of your products, to test
6. Would you please arrange for a representative

4

Beispiellösung

NS / Ihre Anfangsbuchstaben klein geschrieben
(Datum)

Ro AS
N-6146 Aheim
Norway

Sirs

Product enquiry

We were interested in your advertisement in the European Construction Journal of (date).

We are a leading German construction company based in Essen with operations worldwide. You can find more information about us on our website www.tiefhoch.de.

Could you please send us your current sales brochure, price list and samples of your products to test? We would also be interested to learn about possible discounts, your delivery times and your terms of payment. If your products are competitive, we may buy large quantities.

We look forward to hearing from you soon.

Yours faithfully

(Your name)

5

Beispiellösung

NC /
(Date)

Ms Jane Appleyard
Danbury Windows Ltd
101 Lewes Avenue
London NW3 4WW
England

Dear Ms Appleyard

Product enquiry

We were very interested in your products at the trade fair recently in Birmingham, England.

We are a leading German construction company based in Essen with operations worldwide. You can find more information about us on our website www.tiefhoch.de.

Could you please send us your current sales brochure and price list? We understand that you have a sales office in Germany. Would you also please arrange if possible for a representative to visit us?

Yours sincerely

6

Individuelle Lösungen

Unit 7

A

1

1 *market share*
2 product
3 competitors
4 stood out
5 market research
6 to target
7 target group
8 feature
9 brand image
10 to advertise
11 advertising campaign
12 medium
13 posters
14 press
15 new media

B

1

1. *large (adj.)*
2. famous (adj.)
3. easily (adv.)
4. quickly (adv.)
5. interesting (adj.)
6. amazing (adj.)
7. excellent (adj.)
8. interested (adj.)
9. careful (adj.)
10. carefully (adv.)
11. automatic (adj.)
12. automatically (adv.)
13. extremely (adv.)
14. amazingly (adv.)
15. totally (adv.)
16. incredibly (adv.)
17. lovely (adj.)
18. wonderful (adj.)
19. strange (adj.)
20. fast (adj.)
21. fast (adv.)
22. terrible (adj.)
23. terribly (adv.)
24. fantastic (adj.)
25. simple (adj.)
26. simply, clearly (adv., adv.)
27. fantastically, fast (adv., adv.)
28. easily, complicated (adv., adj.)
29. clever, simply awful, immediately (adj., adv., adj. adv.)
30. immediately, friendly, really funny (adv., adj., adv., adj.)

D

1

1. *a pop-up (ad)*
2. commercial
3. banner ad
4. advergaming
5. poster

2

Beispiellösungen
1. It's a kind of advertisement you find on the internet. It's newer than banner ads and pop-ups. It's a video clip with sound.
2. It's a type of advertising you get in films and on TV shows. Advertisers 'place' products (laptops, cars etc.) in scenes so that people see famous actors with the products.
3. It's a kind of advertising you find on social networking sites – MySpace or Facebook, for example.
4. It's a kind of advertising companies use to tell their existing customers about new products and services. It's normally an email to the customers.
5. It's a kind of advertising we're beginning to see in the street. Advertisers use new technology to run different ads at different times of the day.

3

Beispiellösungen
1. *(I think) it's growing so quickly because* people now spend so much time on the internet and also because of the trend towards online shopping.
2. The main reason why it's important to target specific groups when you advertise is that advertising is expensive. You don't want to waste money with advertisements that target people who won't buy your product. (Another reason is that ads can be very annoying when you're not interested in a product).
3. I think one reason why there's so much advertising in the world is that we live in a consumer society. There is also a lot of advertising because markets are very competitive and advertisers have to work hard to 'grab our attention'.

4

Beispiele
classic, sophisticated, fun, reliable, cutting-edge, pure, tempting, delicious, advanced, cool, amazing, unbelievable, unique, exciting, fresh, rugged, strong, stylish, tasty, easy to use, flexible, ideal (for), fantastic, colourful, stunning, chic, unrivalled, ultrafast …

5

Beispiellösung (DASA)

Product or service
supermarket

Medium
poster or magazine advertisement

Brand image
cheap products, good value for money, not complicated

Device(s)
very simple advertisement, quick to read and understand, large letters and few words, large picture of an 'identification figure' (housewife), woman is smiling (= happy, satisfied)

Target group
Women (probably housewives / mothers)

Your reactions
I don't really like the idea that only 'housewives' shop and look after a family. However, the ad is simple and I think it's effective for the target group.

Video lounge

2

James McHardy
James wanted to buy an iPod. The seller sent him an email and asked for money. James paid £210. The next time James logged on, the seller's account was closed and the seller had vanished (disappeared). James complained to eBay but they refused to refund him (give him his money back). James felt 'gutted'. He was also really angry with eBay because they don't go after (try to find, prosecute) scammers.

Dave Oram
Dave wanted to buy a car for his fiancée. He found the perfect car, checked that everything was OK (e.g. that the car wasn't a stolen car), and emailed the seller. Dave got an email back but it wasn't from eBay, it was a hoax. Dave lost £4,000. He was furious, angry with himself, angry with eBay, and upset because his fiancée wouldn't get the car.

Drew Dyer
Drew wanted to buy a laptop and paid his money through PayPal. He didn't get his computer and PayPal didn't refund all his money. They gave Drew £105, but he was still £300 out of pocket (he had lost £300). He was disgusted. He thought eBay and PayPal would protect him but they didn't. He now thinks it isn't safe to shop on eBay.

3 EXTRA

Beispiellösung

(Email by James McHardy to eBay)

Dear eBay

I am writing to protest about your auction site.

I recently paid £210 for an iPod which was advertised on eBay. However, next time I logged on, the seller's account was closed. Two days later, I contacted you about the problem. You refused to refund me.

I am writing to tell you that I am extremely angry. On your website you say: 'Should something go wrong, eBay is there to help'. It isn't! You allow scammers on your site but don't protect honest people!

Yours faithfully

Unit 8

1

- Anfrage von Estetica SL, Alicante, Spanien. Ansprechspartner: Herr Ernesto Alvarez, Einkaufsabteilung.
- Deutsche und britische Kunden der Firma haben unsere Produkte empfohlen.
- Estetica ist eine Kette von über 40 Schönheitssalons hauptsächlich in Touristenhotels Spanienweit. Zentrale in Alicante.
- Möchten aktuellen Verkaufsprospekt und Preislisten sowie Infos über Rabatte, Zahlungsbedingungen und Lieferzeiten.
- Bitten auch um Muster.
- Firma ist ein bedeutendes Unternehmen in der spanischen Schönheitsindustrie und könnte evtl. große Mengen unserer Produkte kaufen.

2

Individuelle Lösungen

3

1. CPT (Valencia): Carriage Paid To Valencia
2. FAS (Hamburg): Free Alongside Ship at the port of Hamburg
3. FOB (Hamburg): Free On Board at the port of Hamburg
4. DDP: Delivered Duty Paid
5. (1) DEQ (Boston): Delivered Ex Quay at the port of Boston
   (2) CFR (Boston): Cost and Freight to the port of Boston (Bezahlt der Verkäufer auch Versicherung, ist in diesem Falle CIF auch möglich)
6. DES: Delivered Ex Ship

4

Beispiellösungen
If a company gives a customer a large discount, the customer will be more likely to buy the product.
If they get a large discount and if they like the product, the customer will also perhaps recommend the product to others.
If the discount (a firm gives) is too large, however, it won't earn any money and it won't make a profit.

5

(4) We are pleased to offer you a 10% introductory discount (off list price).
(1) Thank you very much for *your enquiry of 3 October.*
(5) For a first order, payment should be made with your order.
(2) Enclosed are our current sales brochure and price list.
(3) All prices are CIP (Valencia).
(8) This quotation is valid for three months.
(9) We assure you that we will deal with your order carefully and promptly.
(6) The goods will be dispatched within 21 days after receipt of order.
(7) As you requested, we are sending you immediately samples of our products to test.
(10) We look forward to hearing from you soon.

6

1. *as follows.*
2. willing, prepared
3. quantity discount
4. immediately on receipt of order
5. interest in our products.
6. do not hesitate to contact / get in touch with us.

7

Dear Mr Alvarez

Thank you very much for your enquiry of 3 October.

Enclosed are our current sales brochure and price list. All prices are CIP (Valencia). We are pleased (willing / prepared) to offer you a 10% introductory discount (off list price). For a first order, payment should be made with your order. The goods will be dispatched within 21 days after receipt of order. As you requested, we are sending you immediately samples of our products to test.

This quotation is valid for three months.

(Thank you again for your interest in our products). We assure you that we will deal with your order carefully and promptly. (If you have any further questions, please do not hesitate to get in touch with us).

We look forward to hearing from you soon.

Yours sincerely

8

1. *Thank you for your letter of 4 October and the samples you sent us.*
2. Please find enclosed our purchase order number 1234.
3. We understand from your offer that all your prices are DDP Aachen.
4. You are willing to offer us a discount of 4%.
5. Payment should be made within 30 days after receipt of order.
6. We can expect delivery of the consignment within 7 days of receipt of order.
7. Your offer is valid for 6 months.
8. We look forward to receiving the goods in time and doing further business with you.

9

1 PURCHASE ORDER
2 DATE
3 CAT No.
4 ITEM
5 QTY
6 PRICE
7 AMOUNT
8 SUBTOTAL
9 LESS 10% INTRODUCTORY DISCOUNT
10 TOTAL

Dear Ms Frowein

Thank for your letter of (7) October and the samples you sent us.

Please find enclosed our purchase order number 70/A/12.

We understand from your offer that all prices are CIP (Valencia). We note that you are prepared to offer us an introductory discount of 10%. (Thank you for this). Payment should be made with (our) order. We can expect delivery of the consignment within 21 days after receipt of order. Your offer is valid for three months.

We look forward to receiving the goods in time and doing further business with you.

Yours sincerely

10

Enquiries	Offers	Orders
If your prices are competitive, we may buy large quantities of your products. Please send us your current sales brochure. We would also like to know more about your terms of payment.	Thank you for your enquiry of 9 January. We are pleased to offer you a trade discount of 5%. We are pleased to quote as follows. We hope that this quotation will come up to your expectations.	Thank you for your catalogue and the samples you sent us. We can expect delivery within one week. We look forward to placing further orders with you in the future. We confirm that you are willing to offer us a trade discount of 5%. Payment should be made within 30 days.

Unit 9

A

1

Down
2 fossil fuels
3 power station
4 atmosphere
5 climate
6 drought
7 temperature
10 biomass
11 emitted
12 windpark
15 extreme
17 nuclear
18 warming

Across
1 safe
8 emissions
9 sustainable
13 dioxide
14 hydroelectric
16 poles
19 greenhouse
20 renewable
21 solar
22 wind
23 famine

B

1

simple present	simple past	*will* future
are placed is produced	were made were built	will be produced will be supplied will be built

present perfect	present continuous
has been used have been constructed have been set	is being used are (now) being built

2

1 *is produced*
2 was discovered
3 were manufactured
4 is being supported
5 have been installed
6 are exported
7 will be produced

3

1. electricity — *is produced*
2. CO_2 — is emitted
3. sea journeys — were made
4. oranges — are grown
5. products — are transported
6. flowers — were produced
7. freight — is transported
8. goods — will be transported
9. wine — is produced

4

1 *have been transported*
2 was invented
3 were named
4 be loaded
5 be transported
6 were invented
7 to be loaded
8 be unloaded
9 to be handled
10 be damaged
11 be stolen
12 to be broken

D

1

Electricity *2c*; CNG/LPG 3a; Ethanol/biofuel 1b

Beispiellösung
them (this type of car / electric cars) is that they produce no CO_2 at all when they are driven. The fuel for them – electricity – comes from power stations which pollute the atmosphere, however. Another disadvantage is that electric cars are slow. The second alternative is CNG (compressed natural gas) or LPG (liquid petroleum gas). The big advantage of these two fuels is that they both produce a lot less CO_2 than 'normal' cars. Another good thing about them is that normal cars can be easily converted to use these fuels. The downside of CNG and LPG is that they still produce some CO_2 and so are not a perfect solution. The third alternative is ethanol and biofuels. These have advantages and disadvantages, too. On the one hand, they are carbon neutral. On the other, however, people in poorer countries grow plants for these fuels when they should grow food.

2 EXTRA

1. b; 2. a; 3.c
4. 1964: the invention of the 'mouse'
   1985: first Microsoft Windows
   1958: first silicon chip
   1981: first home computer
   Bill Gates
5. 1973
   New York
6. c; 7. c; 8. b

3 EXTRA

Individuelle Lösungen

Video lounge

Part 1 of the programme
1.
1 revolution
2 expansion
3 fossil fuels
4 dozen
5 inland windfarms

Beispiellösungen
2.
a We are only recognising now in the 21st century the potential of the wind as a possible solution to the global environmental crisis.
b The windfarm was opened two months ago. The Blyth turbines are the largest offshore turbines in the world. Each turbine can produce electricity for 1,500 homes.
c There are plans for two much larger windfarms off the coast of East Anglia.
d Oil was discovered in the North Sea in the late 1950s and for Britain this was a 'bonanza'. Now Britain could be on the verge of another North Sea bonanza but this time it won't be oil that makes Britain rich, but windpower.

3.
a 40% of all energy to come from wind by 2030.
b Britain is the windiest country in Europe.
c It says that thousands of jobs could be created.

Part 2 of the programme
1.
- People in Britain are being 'conned' about windpower.
- Windfarms look horrible (there's an 'aesthetic' problem).
- Windpower can't compete with nuclear energy or coal, oil and gas because it isn't a continuous source of power (it doesn't produce electricity when the wind isn't blowing or is blowing too fast).

2. a major manufacturer is planning to open the UK's first wind turbine factory in Scotland.

Unit 10

1

1 *with reference to*
2 J-770-M
3 when we opened the container
4 instead of
5 *10* cm
6 that we ordered
7 This is a particular problem for us
8 next Monday
9 we need the packing boxes
10 look into this matter for us
11 replacements
12 what you would like us to do with the incorrect boxes?

2

Individuelle Lösungen

3 EXTRA

How goods can be damaged
torn – *zerrissen*
warped – verzogen
scratched – zerkratzt
bent – verbogen
water-damaged – wasserbeschädigt
cracked – geknackt
corroded – verätzt
damaged in transit – auf dem Transportweg beschädigt

Other problems
don't meet our specifications: entsprechen nicht unseren Spezifikationen / technischen Bedingungen
can't be sold: können nicht verkauft werden
are useless to us: sind für uns nutzlos / unbrauchbar

Late delivery
now 10 days overdue: seit 10 Tagen überfällig
without delay: unverzüglich / ohne Verzug

4

1. *zugeben*
2. um Entschuldigung bitten
3. versichern
4. auf unsere Kosten
5. gezwungen sein
6. stornieren
7. Kiste
8. fällig
9. auf etw. zurückzuführen sein
10. unser Bedauern zum Ausdruck bringen

11. defekt
12. als Zeichen (unseres) guten Willens
13. sofortiger Versand
14. kommt (uns) ungelegen
15. prüfen
16. anstatt
17. (einem Problem) nachgehen
18. sich beschweren
19. Verwechslung
20. wieder gutmachen
21. Ersatzlieferung
22. leicht
23. vorübergehend
24. einem Standard nicht entsprechen

5

Individuelle Lösungen

Unit 11

A

1

1 c; 2 g; 3 o; 4 h; 5 f; 6 j; 7 i; 8 k; 9 b; 10 m; 11 l; 12 e; 13 d; 14 a; 15 n

Individuelle Lösungen

B

1

B Was sich in letzter Zeit geändert hat
C Aktuelle Änderungen, die im Moment ablaufen
D Wie es in der Zukunft weitergeht
A Wie es früher war

2

1 *has changed*
2 were
3 were
4 has declined
5 have disappeared
6 was built
7 are expanding
8 are (also) improving
9 will build
10 will be
11 will attract

3

1. *fewer*
2. less
3. fewer
4. fewer
5. less
6. fewer

4

1. little
2. a few
3. a few
4. little
5. little
6. the most
7. the most, the least

5

Beispiellösungen

1. *number, has declined*
2. number, has increased
3. amount, has decreased
4. amount, has shrunk
5. number, has risen
6. amount, has grown
7. amount, has fallen

D

1

Beispiellösungen

2. Collaborating means that you work with another person – or other people. In other words, you work together – for example, on a project.
3. Another word for a co-worker is a work colleague. In other words, it's a person you work with in the same company, office, factory etc.
4. A blue chip company is basically a company that is large, well-know, has a good reputation and is profitable. An example of a blue-chip company is IBM in the USA or Sony in Japan.
5. Mobile wi-fi technology means technology (like laptops, mobile phones etc.) that don't need wires (they're wireless) and so can be used anywhere. The idea behind them is that people don't have to sit at a desk all the time. They can work away from their desk.
6. Space in offices costs money. It is therefore important to use space as efficiently as possible. Space is 'wasted' when it isn't being used.
7. The workplace is basically the place where people work. Examples are offices, factories, schools and so on. We often talk about 'changes in the workplace', in other words, changes in the places where people work.
8. A formal meeting is basically a meeting where there are rules. There is a chairperson, someone takes notes and writes up minutes, and there is an agenda – a list of points to discuss. The idea behind an informal meeting is that there are no (or fewer rules). An example of an informal meeting is a brainstorming meeting, or when a group of co-workers come together spontaneously to discuss a problem.

2

Unternehmen (Sitz / Produkte / Belegschaft / Geschichte / Umsatz)
Sitz: Winesburg, Ohio, USA – Produkte: Snacks – Belegschaft: mittelständisches Unternehmen mit 750 Beschäftigten – Geschichte: vor 15 Jahren gegründet – Umsatz: über $700 m.

Grundwerte des Unternehmens
sich um seine Belegschaft kümmern – sich um das Produkt kümmern – fleißig sein (Gründer: 'Good old Midwestern values') – Transparenz / Offenheit / gute Kommunikation – keine 'Hierarchie'

Wie realisiert das Unternehmen seine Ziele?
sorgfältiges Aussuchen von 'richtigen' Bewerbern – neue Angestellte lernen die Kultur des Unternehmens von älteren Angestellten

Wie hat die Firmenpolitik des Unternehmens zu seinem geschäftlichen Erfolg beigetragen?
niedrige Fluktuation (für die Firma sehr günstig) – hohe Qualität der Produkte (da Arbeiter sehr engagiert sind) – guter Ruf als eine der Firmen in den Top 100 Places To Work in the USA

3 EXTRA

Beispiellösung Around 6 million Germans are already 'teleworkers' and a new report says that this number will increase dramatically in the coming years. Some forms of telework have increased by 50% in recent years. One reason why telework is increasing is that people can now work with emails and the internet from anywhere in the world. Another reason is that telework helps companies to keep down costs. Telework is also popular with people who want a better work-life balance. The world of work for millions of Germans could soon include telework (working from home), SOHOs (Small Office / Home office), Desk-sharing ('hotelling' for example), and a Workplace On Wheels (when office workers keep their documents etc. in a container that they can roll to any desk in the office). Many large companies in Germany are already doing these things, but there are also critics. Being too flexible can distract workers, and many people also like their desk to be 'a home from home'. Some managers are also worried that they can't check on their workers, and not all companies are investing enough in the necessary computer technology. On balance, it is not likely that all workers will become 'nomads' in the future. (200 words)

Unit 12

1

1 *rely on*	6 cashflow
2 bills	7 invoice
3 expensive	8 settled
4 receive	9 original terms of payment
5 owed to	

2

1. *should have paid*
2. *should have been made*
3. should have settled
4. should have received
5. should have been delivered
6. should have been paid
7. should have told
8. should have been enclosed

3

Writing a reminder

1. with reference to ... Our records show that
2. According to our agreed terms ... payment should have been made
3. for your reference
4. oversight ... overlooked ... look into the matter urgently ... settle your account within the next few days
5. If you have settled the invoice in the meantime ... disregard / ignore ... If you have any questions or concerns regarding payment, please do not hesitate to get in touch with us

Replying to a reminder

1. of 31 April ... delay in paying
2. accounts department ... are off sick ... temporary ... customers
3. deferment / an extension ... in instalments
4. understand ... to continuing to do business with you

4

Beispiellösungen (Reminder 1 / Antwort)

Reminder
Dear Mr Kowalski

Our invoice No. 74451/J

I am writing with reference to our invoice number 74451/J. Our records show that payment is now overdue. Under the terms we agreed when you hired our two minibuses, payment should have been made within 30 days.

I am enclosing a copy of the invoice for your reference.

We are sure you have mistakenly overlooked the invoice but please give it your prompt attention now.

If you have already settled your account in the meantime, please ignore this letter.

We look forward to receiving payment from you very soon.

Yours sincerely

Reply
Dear Mrs Stewart

Your invoice No. 74451/J

Thank your for your letter about invoice number 74451/J. We are sorry that you have had to remind us and I can only apologise for the delay in paying. The delay is due to the fact that we have a large number of people off sick at the moment so that our accounts department can't handle all the work. Payment will, however, now be made immediately.

We trust that you will understand our difficult situation and look forward to doing business with you again in the future.

Yours sincerely

5

- Zahlungsverzug ein ernstes Thema, kann Insolvenz zur Folge haben
- zur Regelung von Zahlungsverzügen brachte die EU 2002 Gesetze heraus, gültig für alle EU Länder
- Firmen dürfen nach Ablauf der Zahlungsfrist Zinsen verlangen
- Zinssätze betragen 7-8% mehr als die gängigen Sätze in den Banken des jeweiligen Landes
- zahlen die Klienten trotz der drohenden Zinsen nicht, so dürfen Firmen die Schulden eintreiben, dabei muss der Kunde die auftretenden Kosten übernehmen
- Möglichkeiten die Schulden einzutreiben:
- 1. über einen Anwalt
- 2. Inkassobüros
- 3. und letzter Ausweg ist vor Gericht zu gehen, was sehr teuer werden kann
- welche Möglichkeit gewählt wird hängt von verschiedenen Faktoren, wie z.B. der Beziehung zum Kunden ab und ob der Kunde grunsätzlich pünkltich zahlt
- zur Unterstützung des Kunden können Ratenzahlungen oder ein Aufschub vereinbart werden
- sollte der Schuldner handlungsunfähig werden kann es passieren, dass Rechungen niemals beglichen werden

6 ROUNDUP

1 c; 2 a; 3 a; 4 c; 5 c; 6 b; 7 b; 8 c

Unit 13

A

1

1	*located*	7	tourist arrivals
2	beaches	8	generated
3	coral	9	seasons
4	scuba diving	10	average temperatures
5	destination	11	accommodation
6	income	12	market

2 EXTRA

Individuelle Lösung

B

1

2. the company specialised in cycling holidays for younger people.
3. holidays lasted between four and nine days. People travelled in groups of about ten.
4. GBB arranged accommodation each night and transported people's luggage.
5. last year, GBB had arranged over 1,500 holiday tours (and that) all had been very successful.
6. in August last year, a well-known German travel magazine had given GBB an award for Best Customer Service By A Small Company.
7. She said that the market for cycling holidays in Germany was growing constantly.
8. She told them that cycling holidays were becoming more and more popular.
9. She said that in the last five years, the market had grown by almost 70%.
10. She added that it would certainly grow more in the future.
11. She emphasised that GBB would continue to be a major player in the future.
12. She suggested that British cyclists would love cycling in Germany.

2

1. *GBB offers a range of holidays in different locations. Among others, there* are tours of Bavaria, the Black Forest, the River Rhine and Germany's capital city, Berlin. Two years ago, it (we) also started offering tours in Thuringia.
2. Because the target group is younger people, accommodation is usually in guest houses or cheaper hotels. The typical cost of a 7-day tour is around 400 euros. That includes accommodation, food, and hire of the cycles and cycling equipment. Travel to and from Germany itself is not included in the price.
3. For new customers, GBB will offer a discount of 10% on all holidays for the first six months. It (we) will also provide sales brochures in English.

D

1 1 c; 2 d; 3 a; 4 b

2

1. *Travel companies are meeting customer demand for ethical holidays by developing* innovative solutions to holidays.
2. Some responsible tourists are trying to reduce the impact of their holidays on the environment by staying at home or by travelling by train instead of by plane.
3. You can offset your carbon emissions when you fly by paying a little extra when you book a ticket.

(4. Hotels can make sure that the local community benefits from tourism by employing people from their area and (by) using local food.)

3

1 *They can also be eco-friendly by* using bed sheets made from organic cotton *and by* encouraging their guests to use towels more than once.
2 It is helping tourists to understand other cultures better by offering them the chance to stay in a real community and to take part in a proper two-way cultural exchange.
3 It is helping local people by giving them an alternative to logging work. (They now give guided tours to visitors).
4 You can find out about ethical holidays by looking (on the internet, in travel brochures, in magazines etc.) – there is now a flood of interest.

4 EXTRA

Beispiellösungen

1. Companies make sure that people know about their products by advertising them.
2. Companies could reduce the impact of transport on the environment by using other modes of transport – inland waterways and rail transport, for example.
3. Suppliers can attract B2B customers when they write an offer letter by offering discounts, good terms of payment etc.

Individuelle Lösung

Video lounge

2

Section 1

1. He wants us to imagine that it's the year 2050 and that the earth is much warmer because of global warming. The beach we see isn't in the Mediterranean, it's in Britain.
2. The scientist uses a map on a laptop to show how the climate will change by 2050. The Mediterranean will become too hot for tourism. He says this will mean that British people will stay in Britain for their holidays and that people will come to Britain (many from the Mediterranean).

Section 2

3. There will be huge investment (in tourism), enormous hotels and gigantic resorts. He asks: 'Do we want them (the hotels etc.) here (in Britain)?'
4. The man in the pub is for / in favour of developing tourism but he says businesspeople (investors, developers etc.)

must think about the local people in Cornwall not just the tourists who visit (two or three weeks each year). The lady says that Cornwall needs tourism and the money it brings. Places can be regenerated with the money. She thinks Cornwall would die without tourism.

Section 3

5. Positive: The new developments can bring real opportunities for the Cornish tourist industry (e.g. year-round jobs for local people). Negative (Downside): When too many people come it puts strain on the health services (doctors, hospitals), roads (they become clogged), waste and water supplies.

Section 4

6. Winners: British people who can stay in the UK for their holidays. Losers: British people who live near the coast in places where there is massive tourism.
7. The 'mega developments that we've encouraged in other parts of the world' (e.g. the large resorts you find in Spain).

3

Beispiellösung

Tourism has many advantages for a city or a region. It is a huge industry which generates direct and indirect spending. This means that it brings money to a place and this money supports several industries, especially in the service sector. Tourism is 'good news' for hotels, shops, restaurants and many other services. The big disadvantage of tourism is, of course, that it can destroy or (potentially) damage a city or region. If the place is very beautiful, too many tourists can spoil it. Tourism also puts a real strain on the infrastructure – on health care, roads, water and so on. This can mean that the quality of life of the local people declines. Planners must find a good balance between the advantages and disadvantages of tourism before they develop the place where they live.
(135 words)

E

1

1. *in*, on; 2. for; 3. at; 4. to; 5. of; 6. with; 7. in; 8. on; 9. into; 10. for; 11. on; 12. of; 13. of; 14. of; 15. for; 16. in; 17. by; 18. on; 19. in; 20. on; 21. on; 22. in; 23. on; 24. in

2 EXTRA

German tourist industry had a successful summer again this year – increase in tourists to traditional favourites e.g. North Sea Coast, Black Forest, Lake Constance – only Mecklenburg-Vorpommern recorded a loss (reasons: bad weather / increased competition from Poland) – cities most popular again this year with tourists (third of all tourists visited large cities) – most successful cities of all are those which you can fly to with a low-cost airline e.g. Dresden, Cologne, Berlin – tourist arrivals here up between 9 and 11% – positive trend in German tourism due to increased number of short holidays, business trips and event tourism (98 words)

Unit 14

1

1 *I'm sorry*
2 Can I take a message?
3 She's away all week.
4 Could I take your name again?
5 And could you give me the company name again?
6 And can I just take your phone number, please?
7 81-3-4455-3131.
8 And your message is:
9 Can I just check that I've got everything correct?
10 I'll make sure Mrs Lütkemeyer gets your message as soon as she's back in the office.
11 You're welcome.

2

1.
To: Herr Wimmer
Date: 12 March
Time:
Caller: Ms Sangeet Sharma
Company: New Delhi Engineering Ltd.
Phone number: 11-6923345
Message: Ms Sharma needs to speak to you urgently about the delivery of some goods. She'll call back at 9.00 am our time this morning.

2.
To: Herr Wimmer
Date: 12 March
Time:
Caller: Mr Jack Rogers
Company: National Exhibition Centre, Birmingham, England
Phone number: +44 121-780-4141
Message: Please send Mr Wimmer all the details of your stand at the trade fair next month. He needs the information fairly quickly if possible.

3.
To: Herr Wimmer
Date: 12 March
Time:
Caller: Ms Margareta Halvorsen
Company: Stanqvist AB, Kristianstad, Sweden
Phone number: 044 10 13 66
Message: Ms Halvorsen has to cancel your meeting on 4 April. She's sorry but something important has come up. Please let her have some dates when you're free so that you can arrange another meeting.

3.
To: Herr Wimmer
Date: 12 March
Time:
Caller: Mr Mark Gilbert
Company: First Oklahoma Bank
Phone number: You have this
Message: Everything is arranged for your meeting next month. The bank's two representatives will meet you in New York on the 23rd. Mr Gilbert has also got some tickets for the New York Mets baseball game.

3

You	Eschler GmbH. (Your name). Guten Tag.
Caller	Could I speak to Mr Wimmer, please?
You	I'm afraid he isn't in the office today. Can I take a message?
Caller	When will he be back?
You	Not until tomorrow.
Caller	OK. This is Martin Rutherford from UK Wholesale Ltd in London. Could you tell Mr Wimmer that I'm coming to Dusseldorf the week after next and I'd like to meet him? I'll call at the beginning of next week to arrange a time.
You	Could I take your name again, please?
Caller	Rutherford. Martin Rutherford.
You	Would you spell that for me, please?
Caller	Sure. Martin, M-A-R-T-I-N, Rutherford, R-U-T-H-E-R-F-O-R-D.
You	And can I take your phone number, please?
Caller	It's 020 246 4386.
You	Thank you. And your message is: You're coming to Dusseldorf the week after next and you'd like to meet Mr Wimmer. You'll call at the beginning of next week to arrange a time.
Caller	Yes, that's right.
You	Can I just confirm everything? Mr Martin Rutherford from UK Wholesale Ltd, London. Telephone number 020 246 4386. Mr Rutherford is coming to Dusseldorf the week after next and would like to meet you. He'll telephone at the beginning of next week to arrange a time for the meeting.
Caller	Great.
You	I'll make sure Mr Wimmer gets your message as soon as he comes in, Mr Rutherford.
Caller	Thanks very much for your help. Bye.
You	You're welcome. Goodbye.

4 EXTRA

2. Sierra – Charlie – Hotel – Mike – India – Delta – Tango
3. Kilo – Oscar – Echo – Lima – November
4. Zulu – India – Mike – Mike – Echo – Romeo – Mike – Alpha – November – November

Individuelle Lösungen

5 ROUNDUP

1 c; 2 c; 3 a; 4 c; 5 c; 6 b; 7 a; 8 c; 9 a; 10 c

Unit 15

A

1

1. *American*, European, Indian, Chinese, Cambodian, Ugandan, Amazonian, American
2. Japanese
3. Japanese
4. Brazilian
5. Thai, Thai
6. Kenyans, Ugandans
7. Pakistani
8. Lebanese

B

1

2. Could you tell me if the plane to Bangkok is on time, please?
3. Could you tell me where I can get a taxi, please?
4. Could you tell me what time breakfast is, please?
5. Could you tell me how I phone Germany from my hotel room, please?
6. Could you tell me if you have internet access in all the rooms, please?
7. Could you tell me if there's a good restaurant near here, please?
8. Could you tell me if your office is in the city centre, please?
9. Could you tell me what Mr Tanaka's cell phone number is, please?
10. Could you tell me where the women's toilets are, please?
11. Could you tell me how big your product range is, please?
12. Could you tell me when you're visiting Germany, please?

2

2. think
3. thought, don't think
4. means
5. meant

D

1

Positive: *(quite) acceptable*, brilliant, encouraging, excellent, understandable, wonderful
Negative: appalling, awful / terrible, crazy / stupid, depressing, disappointing, disgusting, ridiculous, sad, strange / odd, surprising, unacceptable, unbelievable

2

Beispiellösungen

2. I think it's brilliant / wonderful that clothes in our shops are cheaper now than ever before.
3. I think it's awful / unacceptable / disgusting / unbelievable that Jivaj works around 12 hours a day and sometimes more.
4. I think it's encouraging that things have certainly improved.
5. I think it's depressing / disappointing that it's almost impossible to track down all of the sweatshops.
6. I think it's understandable / quite acceptable that all businesses try to make the biggest possible profit.

Individuelle Lösungen

3

2. The Fairtrade organisation was formed by combining the work of a number of different groups who were all already active in developing countries.
3. The main idea behind the Fairtrade organisation is to get a better deal for farmers and others in developing countries.
4. The main reason why the organisation is necessary in today's global world is that there is such an unfair balance in world trade. In other words, in the global economy it is the rich nations that control trade.
5. A 'stable price' is basically a price that doesn't go up or down – it stays the same for a long time. The reason why

a stable price is important is that it allows farmers to invest in their farms and to plan long-term.

6. Fairtrade helps farmers in the Developing World (first) by finding business partners in the Developed World who sell Fairtrade goods and (second) by guaranteeing a fixed, minimum price for goods.
7. The downside of Fairtrade is that Fairtrade goods are sometimes a little more expensive. However, that isn't really a major problem because people in Europe want to help the farmers (so they're willing / prepared to pay extra).
8. The 'Fairtrade mark' is a kind of logo that you find on the packaging of all Fairtrade products.
9. The first reason why the mark is so important is that it guarantees / reassures consumers that money really goes to farmers in developing countries. The second is that it also guarantees / reassures consumers that products really come from Fairtrade farmers.
10. It is the FLO (Fairtrade Labelling Organisation) based in Bonn in Germany that checks that the mark is valid. The good thing about that system is that it is independent (so people trust it).

Video lounge

2

Economic reasons for child labour in the Ivory Coast
The Ivory Coast supplies half the world's cocoa but there is stagnation everywhere – adult workers barely earn £100 a year – situation hasn't changed for 30 years

The 'Cocoa Protocol' – When? Who? Why?
2001 – chocolate industry (promised to start eradicating child labour) – reason: international outcry

Marc's father and life in Marc's village
Kanga John Kwame father of Marc and his brother Fabrice – teaches the boys to work the land – explains life is poor and they have no money – life very hard in the village – everywhere boys with wounds from machetes – no medicine for treatment

Marc's story
Father took Marc out of school to work – hasn't seen mother for 10 years

The BBC reporter's question to the viewers at the end
Why is Marc so poor when the chocolate industry generates billions of pounds a year? Who can help Marc: father, billionaire chocolate business, us the consumers?

3

Beispiellösung
In this video called 'Cocoa Children' a reporter from the BBC visits the Ivory Coast, the West African country which supplies half the world's cocoa. He wants to find out about child labour on the country's cocoa farms. Cocoa workers are extremely poor and that's the reason why children have to work on the farms. In 2001, the chocolate industry promised to start eradicating child labour. The reporter finds, however, that child labour still goes on. He visits a plantation where he meets two 12-year-old brothers, Marc and Fabrice, and their father. The two boys work on the plantation because the father is so poor. In the village, the reporter finds other boys like Marc. Many have wounds from machetes. Marc tells the reporter that he used to go to school, but his father took him out. The video is very shocking and at the end the reporter asks an important question: Who can help Marc? (156 words)

E

1

Down		Across	
1	look forward to	3	come / came across
2	gave away	4	lay off
3	called off	5	check in
6	get on with	9	come up with
7	turned down	11	looks after
8	sort out	13	turned up
10	broke down	15	put up with
12	hold on	17	find out
14	put up	19	give out
16	took up		
18	set up		

Unit 16

1 **A letter of enquiry**

Beispiellösung

Dear Sirs

Product enquiry

We recently saw your products at the Cleaning Industry Exhibition in Brussels.

We are a medium-sized manufacturer of road sweeping vehicles (based in) (Dusseldorf) in Germany. You can find more information about us on our website www.reincom.de.

We are always interested in new, environmentally friendly products. Could you please send us your current sales brochure and price list? We would also be interested to learn about (possible) discounts and your delivery times.

We look forward to hearing from you soon.

Yours faithfully

2 **An offer**

Beispiellösung

Dear Mr Dover

Offer

Thank you for your letter of (date). We are pleased to quote as follows.

Enclosed is our current price list. All prices are CIF Harwich. (Please note that) we prefer to send our consignments by inland waterway and by maritime transport as these are cost effective and environmentally friendly. We are willing to offer a quantity discount of 5% on orders over €5,000. For a first order, our normal terms of payment are (we always require) payment with your order. Delivery will be made within 14 days of receipt of order.

This offer is valid for 6 months.

Thank you again for your interest in our products. We are sure that you will be very satisified with the quality of our wines. If you have any further questions, please do not hesitate to contact us.

Yours sincerely

3 An order

Beispiellösung

Dear Ms Ellis

Purchase order No. 4422

Many thanks for your offer and (for) the samples you sent us.

We are satisfied with the quality of the products and enclosed you will find our purchase order No. 4422.

We would like to confirm that all prices are DDP Frankfurt. We (also) note that you are prepared to offer us an introductory discount of 10%. Payment should be made within 30 days of receipt of the consignment. Delivery will be made within 7 days.

We look forward to receiving the goods in time and doing further business with you (in future).

Yours sincerely

4 A complaint

Beispiellösung

Dear Ms Lundgren

I'm afraid I have to write to you about our order number 00-A-134. The goods reached us (arrived) yesterday. However, when we opened the container, we found (discovered) that there were two problems. First, all (the) items in crate no. 3 were badly damaged. Second, crate no. 4 contained black tables instead of the white tables that we had ordered.

This is very inconvenient for us as we have advertised (promoted) your products in the last two weeks. Some of our best customers are already interested in them. Moreover, we are known for our quality and (good) service.

Could you please look into this problem immediately? Please send us replacements urgently. Please (also) let us know what you would like us to do (what we should do) with the damaged and incorrect goods.

Yours sincerely

5 A reminder

Beispiellösung

Dear Mr Roberts

Our invoice No. 817496

Please note that we have not yet received payment for our invoice no. 817496. Payment should have been made within 14 days.

I am enclosing a copy of the invoice for your convenience (for your reference).

This is probably a simple oversight but we would ask you to settle your account within the next few days.

If you have already settled the invoice in the meantime, please disregard (ignore) this reminder.

We look forward to an early settlement of your account and to doing business with you in the future.

Yours sincerely

Practice Exam 1

Teil 1 Hörtext

Good afternoon, this is a message for Aino Soderlund in the sales department. Aino, this is Jack Dewey from Waterstone Inc. in Cleveland, Ohio. It's Friday, 5th April, early afternoon your time. Of course you do remember that I am coming over to see your new 260 XTD which you told me about on the phone last week, do you?

Unfortunately, there's been a slight change in my plans for my trip to Europe in two weeks' time. As I can only see the head of our French sales office on Tuesday instead of Monday, I will be arriving in Finland a day later, on Wednesday. It's a very important meeting in Paris about our latest sales figures, so I can't stick to our original plans. Sorry about that.

The new arrangement means that my flight from Paris arrives in Helsinki on Wednesday at 17:05 (flight number AF 2435). Could you meet me at the airport? And could you please change the booking for my hotel? I'll stay at the same hotel, the Loimaa Business Hotel, from Wednesday 23rd October to Friday 25th.

And one more thing: we will need to discuss the 360 TD. We've had some complaints from important customers lately. Maybe you could ask your production manager to join our meeting? OK, that's it for today. I'm really looking forward to seeing you on the 23rd then. Have a nice weekend and give my regards to your family.
Bye!

DATE *5 October 20___*

MESSAGE FOR *Aino Soderlund*

TOPIC / CONTRACT / SUBJECT *Mr Dewey's visit to see 260 XTD*

Mr/Ms *Jack Dewey* of *Waterstone Inc. in Cleveland, Ohio called.*

S/he ☐ wants you to call back on ____________
☐ will call back again later
☒ left the following message:

He will arrive here a day later (on Wednesday, 23rd April) because he needs to see the head of the French sales office on Monday;

His flight from Paris arrives in Helsinki at 17:05 (flight number AF2435). Could you meet him at the airport?

Could you change the booking for his hotel? He will stay at the Loimaa Business Hotel from Wednesday 23rd to Friday 25th October.

He would also like to discuss some details of the 360 TD with you because of some recent complaints from his customers. He also suggests that our production manager takes part in the meeting.

MESSAGE TAKEN BY *Simone*

Teil 2 Mediation

The German company Lagenfeld Karosseriebau is a medium-sized producer of specialist car bodies. They have 65 employees, their headquarters and production facilities are in Frankfurt/Main.

With 40 years of experience in the production of car bodies they have made an international name and sell their high-quality products all over the world. Their main area of activity is the production of car bodies for commercial vehicles according to customers' wishes. For example: heavy-duty haulage trucks, multi-purpose vehicles, all-terrain vehicles or auto cranes.

Before the actual production of the car bodies begins, their R&D specialists work closely together with their customers to make sure that all details and requirements are met. Even after the car bodies are delivered, Lagenfeld Karosseriebau provides further customer service.

Lagenfeld Karosseriebau can be contacted by phone (069 44104373-0) or mail (info@Lagenfeld-karosseriebau.de).

Teil 3 Rezeption Leseverstehen

Aspect	Information from the text
TMFs in general (product description)	• mounted on the rear of a truck • can be dismounted in less than a minute • make the transport of any kind of goods fast and convenient • can lift up to 3.5 tonnes
TMF producers	• world's biggest TMF producers are in Ireland and in the USA. • both are part of Hiab Oy, a company owned by Cargotec Corp of Helsinki, Finland
TMF markets	• market size: 6,000 units annually • 50% of the units are sold in North America, 2,000 TMFs are bought in Europe • the industry is intensely competitive • USA: building materials industry is TMF industry's most important customer; 70% per cent of the forklift sales

Teil 4 Produktion schriftlich

(Verfassen eines englischsprachigen Briefes nach Stichworten)

Rino Lifts Oy

VisionScan Ltd,
35 Belgrave Road,
Nottingham
NG5 9RA
UK. ______________________, 20___

Dear Sir or Madam

Enquiry for document scanners and document management software

As a medium-sized Finnish producer of truck-mounted lifts we are currently planning to move towards a paperless office. Therefore we are looking for a supplier of document scanners and document management software.

We found the name and address of your company on the internet and would like to ask for further information about the scanners and the software you offer. Could you please send us your latest catalogue and price list?

The scanners we are looking for should be fast, reliable and easy to use. Installation should also be simple. Furthermore, we would appreciate a seminar in which you introduce us to the scanners and the document management software.

If your prices are competitive we would consider ordering 75 scanners together with the management software.

We look forward to hearing from you soon,

Yours faithfully

Rino Lifts Oy

Teil 5 Produktion eigene Stellungnahme

Pro	Kontra
Die Entscheidungen sind langfristig und nicht nur ein Modetrend.	Viele Kunden treffen eine Kaufentscheidung über den Preis. 7% mehr ist eine deutliche Preiseerhöhung.
Können wirklich etwas verändern.	Rino Lift riskiert mit diesen Maßnahmen die Arbeitsplätze von einigen Mitarbeitern.
Das Image von Rino Lifts wird sich bei guter Kommunikationspolitik des Unternehmens verbessern.	Dese Maßnahmen verlangen sehr umfangreiche Investitionen.
Die Entscheidungen beziehen sich auf wesentliche Bereiche des Umweltschutzes: Transport und Energie. Das sind wichtige Entscheidungen mit Vorbildcharakter.	Die ersten beiden Maßnahmen werden sich erst nach einigen Jahren positiv auswirken, kosten aber heute schon.
Ein Preisanstieg von 7% ist vertretbar, wenn man ihn den Kunden ordentlich erklärt.	...
...	...

Practice exam 2

Teil 1 REZEPTION mündlich (Hörverstehen)

Hörtext:

Playlearn Limited is a producer of educational toys with its headquarters in Hong Kong. Founded in 1981, the company is run by two former teachers who have specialized in inventing toys for children all around the world. The company has grown considerably over the last ten years and now has customers and distributors on all five continents. Currently they sell most of their products to the USA and Great Britain, but other European countries, especially the Scandinavian ones, are catching up as well. Primary schools, kindergartens and families buy the toys made in Hong Kong.

Playlearn gives high priority to communication with its customers: they are constantly looking for new ways to get detailed feedback on their toys. Families are also offered prizes, discounts and other extras if they come up with new ideas for toys and games. They encourage children to actively take part in developing the company's product range.

Until recently Playlearn concentrated on board games, puzzles and dolls, but they have now started a new range of electronic educational toys as well. These include building kits, memories and musical instruments. Their latest product is an exciting new Kids' Computer. This has a modern, colourful but robust design, with a child-friendly keyboard and mouse as well as a large screen. The computer comes with more than 30 exciting educational games and activities which aim at improving a child's skills in speaking, writing, mathematics and logic. It runs on batteries or mains electricity.

Aspect	Information
the company	• producer of educational toys with its headquarters in Hong Kong • founded in 1981 • run by two former teachers • specialized in inventing toys for children all around the world • has grown considerably over the last ten years
its customers	• sell most of their products to the USA and Great Britain, but other European countries, especially the Scandinavian ones, are catching up as well • schools, kindergartens and families buy the toys made in Hong Kong. • customers and distributors on all five continents
product range	• board games, puzzles and dolls • electronic educational toys • building kits, memories and musical instruments
product development	• families are also offered prizes, discounts and other extras if they come up with new ideas for toys and games • they encourage children to actively take part in developing the company's product range
the new Kids' Computer	• modern, colourful but robust design • child-friendly keyboard, mouse • large screen • more than 30 exciting educational games and activities which aim at improving a child's skills in speaking, writing, mathematics and logic • runs on batteries or mains electricity

Teil 2 Rezeption Leseverstehen

Aspect	Information
Marketing facts, new developments	• increased trend of marketing to kids and teenagers • marketing to kids used to concentrate mainly on sweets and toys • now it includes computer and entertainment products, clothes and shoes, fast food, sports equipment etc • even advertising for products such as cars, holidays or credit cards aimed at children
Main points of criticism	• question: are children able to understand what advertising is? • children can easily be influenced by advertisers • advertising campaigns encourage children to find happiness and self esteem through consumption
Reasons why children are targeted	• children spend a huge amount of money (more than $100 billion each year) • children have an influence on their parents spending • children will spend money when they grow up (brand loyalties and consumer habits are formed when children are young)

Teil 3 MEDIATION

For the toys market in Germany the last weeks of the year mean a time of intense competition because more than 40 percent of the branch's annual turnover is made at this time. Consequently, retailers and wholesalers have to prepare well for this period. To achieve the best possible results, companies need a comprehensive package of measures, for example:

- an attractive and up-to-date range of products which attract customers,
- a clever marketing strategy, tailor-made for different target groups,
- flexible discounts to meet local requirements.

In cooperation with the biggest toy manufacturers, large national chain stores launch advertising campaigns on TV. Special TV spots are produced to present the season's highlights. Moreover, there is a variety of catalogues (both complete catalogues and theme catalogues) which can be picked up in shops or which are sent by post. Finally, there are numerous competitions where attractive prizes can be won.

Teil 4 Produktion schriftlich

(Verfassen eines englischsprachigen Briefes nach Stichworten)

Toysworld GmbH
Playlearn Ltd
21/F, One Kowloon,
1 Wang Yuen Street,
Kowloon Bay,

Hong Kong ______________________, 20__

Dear Sir or Madam

Enquiry for Kid's Computer

We are a medium-sized German wholesaler of toys and educational articles. We mainly operate in Germany and other German speaking European countries.

We recently listened to a radio documentary in which your latest product, the Kid's Computer, was introduced. As we believe that this product might sell well on our market, we would like to receive further information. Could you please send us your sales literature and your current price lists? Furthermore, could you please send us two computers so that we can test them?

As you are surely aware that the toys market is an extremely competitive market, we can only consider goods of premium quality at competitive prices. Should your computer meet these requirements, regular orders in the future are quite likely.

However, should we decide to do business together we would expect to be the exclusive German importer of the new computer. I hope that this is acceptable to you. Please let us know your view.

We look forward to hearing from you soon.

Yours faithfully

Toysworld GmbH

Teil 5 Produktion eigene Stellungnahme

Pro	Kontra
Produkt ist für Kinder hergestellt; also sollte auch die Zielgruppe beworben werden.	An Kinder gerichtete Werbung kann innerhalb der Zielgruppe zu einem Druck führen, das Produkt zu kaufen, um so innerhalb der Gruppe anerkannt zu sein.
Erst wenn durch die Werbung in der Zielgruppe der Kinder ein Bedarf geweckt ist, werden sich die Eltern mit einem solchen Produkt auseinander setzen.	Kinder können nicht mehr zwischen wirklichem Bedarf und materiellem Überfluss unterscheiden.
In einer Marktwirtschaft werden Kaufanreize mehrheitlich durch Werbung hervorgerufen, das gilt auch für Kinder.	Können sich nicht mit dem Produkt und seinen Features auseinandersetzen und eine informierte Kaufentscheidung treffen, sie „wollen" auch diesen Computer, weil sie alles wollen, was beworben wird.
...	Werbung, die an Kinder gerichtet ist, gibt kaum Informationen, sondern nur Kaufanreize.
...	Eltern sollten sich aufgrund der Werbung über das Produkt informieren können; weil sie die Kaufentscheidung treffen müssen, sollte auch die Werbung an sie gerichtet sein.

Practice exam 3

Teil 1 REZEPTION mündlich (Hörverstehen)

Hörtext:

Hi, my name is Piet, this is Maryum and this is Ninette. We are the fashion label BBB WorldWear. We make modern, comfortable and young leisure wear for men and women. It's a new street style which we most of all consider global. That means that people from all over the world can and of course should buy our fashion.

But global also means that our origins are global. BBB stands for the countries we come from: Belgium, Bangladesh and Burundi. Three countries, three continents. So we can say that we truly represent influences from all over the world. When we decided that we wanted to start our own label, we first travelled to all our home countries to see how the people live in that part of the world. This way we understood each other better.

We all met at the London Fashion School and decided that we wanted to produce our own style. Of course we know that this is very difficult in today's extremely competitive fashion world but we are optimistic. Newcomers *can* be successful and get their products into fashion stores.

What makes us different is the wide range of influences and styles we work with. There are traditional African fashion elements, modern Western styles but also traces of ancient Asian garments to be found in our work. We are confident that we will find buyers for our products after the success of our recent fashion shows.

Our clothes will be made in factories in Bangladesh and in Burundi. For us this has two advantages: on the one hand, production costs in these parts of the world are lower, which means that our clothes are affordable. On the other hand – and this is the strongest argument – we give work to people in our countries. We keep tight control over the production process, making sure that the people who work for BBB WorldWear are not exploited. If we are successful, our countries and the regions we come from will benefit from our success. For some people this will mean that life will be very different from that of their parents. For example ...

Teil 2 Rezeption Leseverstehen

Aspect	Information
Production	• in almost every country in the world various types of clothes are produced • many multinational clothing manufacturers have decided to move their production facilities to places with lower working standards • countries like China, Bangladesh, and Honduras are among the most popular • China is the largest exporter of fast fashion, accounting for 30% of world fashion exports
Employment	• fashion industry is the largest source of industrial employment in the world • about 30 million people are making clothes and textiles across the globe • often there are lower wages and poor conditions for workers • scarcity of alternative employment in these countries
Ecology	• textile production leaves a large pollution footprint • demand for energy-intensive polyester has nearly doubled in the last 15 years • a quarter of all the pesticides used in the United States is used for cotton

Teil 3 MEDIATION

Heek & Treckendorf is a multinational company which is listed on the stock exchange. In order to operate profitably, they must be part of the global supply networks. If they want to offer competitive prices to their customers, they need to search worldwide for the most favourable prices for supplies and products.

The search for new suppliers and manufacturers, particularly in Asia, has increased Heek & Treckendorf's margins by 10–